20th Century
SCOTTISH BANKNOTES
Volume II

20th Century
SCOTTISH BANKNOTES

A detailed review and catalogue of notes issued by the Scottish banks
during the present century.

JAMES DOUGLAS

(completed by Robert W. Pringle)

Volume 2

The Royal Bank of Scotland plc and its constituent banks

The Commercial Bank of Scotland Limited

The National Bank of Scotland Limited

National Commercial Bank of Scotland Limited

The Royal Bank of Scotland

Published by Banking Memorabilia
P.O. Box 14
Carlisle CA3 8DZ

British Library Cataloguing in Publication Data

Douglas, James
20th Century Scottish Banknotes
Volume 2
The Royal Bank of Scotland plc and its
constituent banks

The Commercial Bank of Scotland Limited
The National Bank of Scotland Limited
National Commercial Bank of Scotland Limited
The Royal Bank of Scotland

ISBN   0   947797   025   Bound
          0   947797   033   Limp
Volume 1 published 1984
Volume 3 in preparation
Text set in 10 on 12pt Times New Roman
Tables set in 8pt on 11pt Times New Roman

FIRST PUBLISHED 1986

Banking Memorabilia

© 1986

Printed in Great Britain
by Charles Thurnam & Sons Ltd., Carlisle.

Banknote Photography by R. S. Taylor,
Musselburgh, Scotland.

Colour Origination by
Spectrum Pre Print Ltd., Carlisle.

JAMES DOUGLAS

The author of this book, James Douglas, died on 20th February, 1985. With his death there was lost to Scotland the outstanding pioneer, dedicated researcher, and world authority in the whole field of Scottish banknote issues and history. His earlier work, **"Scottish Banknotes"** published in 1975, became the standard reference work on the subject and his Volume I of the present series, published in 1984, was an instant success, representing as it does the most detailed study of its kind anywhere in the world.

Whereas James Douglas had been a banker in Scotland with The Commercial Bank, the National Commercial Bank and latterly The Royal Bank from 1928 until his retirement in 1972, at the time of his death he was both Curator of the Note Collection of the Institute of Bankers in Scotland and Archivist to the Bank of Scotland. Those who knew him well benefited greatly not only from his immense store of knowledge, but from his gentle charm and great kindness. His insistence on meticulous accuracy in his chosen field established standards which will be with us for many years.

Before his death he had written four-fifths of the manuscript for Volume II of this series and had discussed many aspects of it with me over a number of years. With the kind permission of his widow Joan, I have undertaken the completion of the manuscript and its bringing to publication; full responsibility thus rests with me for all errors and omissions in substance, layout, and proof reading, particularly in the sections devoted to The Royal Bank and The National Bank where much research remained to be done.

However, the manuscript could not have been completed without enthusiastic help from the staff of The Royal Bank of Scotland plc, including Miss Christina H. Robertson, Librarian and Archivist (who found for me the important missing Royal Bank note records) and Mr. M. Sinclair, the Assistant Cashier. Thanks are also due to Mr. J. T. Spears, the Chief Cashier, for much help and for granting permission to include illustrations of the various notes, and to his predecessors in that Office, Mr. J. M. Sanders and Mr. C. S. Rutherford, for their kind co-operation. The interest of Sir Michael Herries, Chairman of the Bank, has been a great encouragement.

Robert W. Pringle

INTRODUCTION TO VOLUME II

Volume I of **"20th Century Scottish Banknotes"** deals in detail with the note issues of the Bank of Scotland and its constituent banks, The British Linen Bank and The Union Bank of Scotland Limited. In the same manner Volume II outlines the banknotes issued during the present century by The Royal Bank of Scotland plc together with those of its constituents. Where possible official records have been consulted and much information on the attractively-designed notes is made available to collectors for the first time.

THE
PREFACE.

THE following Sheets are for the most part only a Narrative of Matters of Fact, which at first were begun, and for many Years carried on for private Use only, without any Thought that they would be continued to a Time when it would be useful to publish them:

It is the Practice of the present Age to let nothing pass on any Subject almost, however well said and true, without an Answer and Censure; and I believe what I now publish will raise the Spirits of more than one. Whoever shall take the Trouble of writing against me, if they do it by Railery and stretching Wit, which now a Days is common in the Defence of bad Causes, or if they do it with Malice, which Party and Faction has nourished to a monstruous Pitch; I shall not in the least regard what they say: But if any Thing shall be said to convince me of a Mistake in my Way of reasoning, I shall willingly own my Error; or if any Thing shall be offered for rectifying me in any Facts, I shall not obstinately persist in a Mistake.

It is very probable my Narrations will by some be slighted, as of little Use and not worth noticing, whether right or wrong; whoever shall be pleased to do so, as he will not thereby make me uneasy,

The anonymous author of "An Historical Account of the Establishment, Progress and State of the Bank of Scotland" published in 1728.

Some two and a half centuries have passed but the author of this present work finds much in the above Preface to merit its reproduction here.

GENERAL INTRODUCTION

"Scottish Banknotes" published by Stanley Gibbons Publications Limited in December 1975 covers the whole field of Scottish note issues since 1695. Although a "pioneer" work it has been accepted as the standard reference book on the subject and in addition to providing a catalogue of the notes contains much historical background to this fascinating series. Considerable space was of necessity devoted to 18th and 19th century issues which nowadays are all too seldom available to collectors. With the issues of the present century providing the bulk of the material available on the market numerous requests have been received by the author to prepare a new work covering such issues in greater detail. This then, is an attempt to meet the needs of collectors wishing information in greater depth on "modern" issues than was possible in "Scottish Banknotes."

This additional information has been gleaned from several sources and where possible the official bank records have been consulted. These records, however, omit many of the details sought by collectors — changes in the signing officials to quote an example — and recourse has been made to the actual notes held in private and institutional collections to fill the gaps.

In spite of the wealth of information contained in the following pages it would be foolish to suggest that they represent the final word on the subject. The opportunity still exists for the keen collector to uncover the "unrecorded," but surely it is this prospect which encourages him to continue to research his chosen field. The author, with due modesty, can but claim to have recorded all the information which, at the time of writing, was available to him.

THE CATALOGUE

Scope. Listing is confined to the issues of the Twentieth Century, each bank commencing with the designs or modifications to an existing design appearing around the year 1900.

Information Columns.   Details of each note are listed as follows.

Column 1. **Type Reference Number:**
The relative reference number in "Scottish Banknotes."

Column 2. **Sub-type Reference Number:**
Applicable to the various sub-types.

Column 3. **Dates:**
Printed dates on the notes. Actual dates of issue may be anything up to three years later.

Column 4. **Serial Letters/Numbers.**

Column 5. **Numbers Printed:**
Where quoted they have been extracted from official records.

Column 6. **Valuation:**
The price which a collector may reasonably be asked to pay. Earlier notes are quoted in the lower grades only. Top grade example of such notes are rare and command high prices when they appear on the market. "Specimen" notes are quoted in E.F. condition only. See paragraph on Condition.
Valuations are those at the date of publication and readers should allow for subsequent fluctuation.

Sizes and Formats of the Scottish Notes

Variations in the sizes of the notes, resulting from successive reductions in the formats, fall neatly into categories. There are four distinct sizes for the One Pound notes, and four for those of the higher denominations. As each size is visually identifiable there is no need to quote exact dimensions against the individual notes listed in the catalogue, the various sizes being denoted by reference letters A B C and D for the One Pound notes and W X Y and Z for the others. The system was introduced by the author in an article in "Coin Year Book 1972" and is used in "Scottish Banknotes." It has now been universally adopted by collectors and dealers. For the most part the sizes correspond to those of Bank of England notes issued since 1928, although the dates of introduction of the various sizes are earlier than those of the English series.

The sizes are as follows, the dimension given being regarded as "average," as minor variations occur between the issues of different banks.

One Pound Notes

Millimetres

Size A.	174 x 128	Until 1929. Often referred to as the old "square notes."
Size B.	152 x 84	From 1924. Similar to the Bank of England One Pound note of 1928.
Size C.	151 x 71	From 1961. Similar to the contemporary Bank of England note.
Size D.	135 x 67	From 1968. The current size, and similar to that introduced by the Bank of England in 1978.

Other Denominations

Size W.	206 x 130	In use by some of the banks until 1970. Similar to the old Bank of England "white" notes.
Size X.	182 x 99	A transitional size for £5 notes, but currently used for £20 and £100 notes.
Size Y.	158 x 89	1961. Transitional for £5 notes and later adopted for some £10 notes.
Size Z.	146 x 78	From 1966. Current size of £5 notes and similar to that introduced by the Bank of England in 1971.

4

Positional Code Letters

Keen-eyed collectors have detected minute letters concealed within the design margin on the lower left-hand corners of notes printed by Waterlow & Sons Ltd. These are to be found not only on Scottish notes, but also on those of other countries printed by Waterlow from multiple plates. They have been wrongly described as "plate numbers" but these, normally five-figure numbers, are to be found on the margin of the printed sheet. In fact the minute letters are code letters identifying the position on the multiple sheet of each individual note impression in much the same manner and for the same purpose as the corner letters on the early British line-engraved stamps. Where several multiple plates were in use over the period of a particular issue, the code letters were modified by the addition of symbols (e.g. a period or a dash) applicable to each plate. This whole subject has yet to be studied in depth and it is sufficient for the general collector to be aware of their presence. For the specialist, however, there is great scope for further research. It is possible for him to reconstruct the plate from the code letters on individual notes in the same way as philatelists have for long reconstructed stamp plates. In fact the task of the note collector should be that much easier. He has only to deal with sheets of 16 or 20 impressions at most, while his philatelic colleague has to contend with sheets of up to 240 stamps. Positional code letters are also present on the back designs.

Code letters are to be found on the Waterlow printings of the following Scottish issues.

The British Linen Bank
The Commercial Bank of Scotland Limited
The National Bank of Scotland Limited
The Union Bank of Scotland Limited.

A	E
B	F
C	G
D	H

A	E	I	M
B	F	J	N
C	G	K	O
D	H	L	P

SOME GUIDELINES ON COLLECTING
20th CENTURY SCOTTISH NOTES

Collectors must always feel free to collect just what they want, and in the manner which appeals to them. By adhering to this adage the collection will assume a character which reflects the individuality of the owner. Having said this there can be no harm in highlighting some points which may influence, and perhaps assist, collectors of this series.

Condition: Of course we all like to have our notes in uncirculated condition, and with recent issues there is no reason why such a standard cannot be maintained. It will soon become apparent to the collector, however, that he may have to lower his sights considerably in acquiring pre-1930 notes. Indeed, pre-1914 notes have become "collectable" in virtually any condition! The collector who turns up his nose at a tatty Commercial Bank note of the "black" issue of 1907, or a Royal Bank £ 10 note of series C, will probably live to regret the lost opportunity of acquiring such a rarity, as he may never see one again let alone be offered one.

Signatures, Dates and Serials: Collectors new to the Scottish series will almost certainly concentrate first on building up a "type" collection before venturing into the realms of signatures, dates, and serial letters. Confusion may arise regarding allocation of priorities to the various areas when expanding the collection. Popular choice seems to favour the signature variations within particular issues and completion in this field should not prove too difficult to achieve, at least in the One Pound denomination. Dates rank next in importance. On occasion — as with the current Royal Bank and Clydesdale series — the date is an integral part of the engraved plate and changes can be classed as plate variations. Some banks — notably The British Linen Bank and The Bank of Scotland — had frequent date changes during certain periods, but generally the changes take place on an annual or biennial basis.

Serial letters and numbers (the official terms used by both the banks and the printing establishments, and adopted here in preference to the word "prefix", which has recently crept into the collectors' vocabulary) are always added to notes after printing. They sometimes figure prominently in dealers' lists largely as a "rub-off" from the Bank of England series, which omit dates, and in which the collector has no option but to concentrate on serials in the course of expanding his collection.

Gimmics: First and last serial letters, low numbers etc. are best regarded as "fun things." Yes, they do have a following, particularly in the field of overseas issues, but the Scottish series offers the general collector so much by way of genuine variety to risk being bogged down by features which really only justify the attention of a specialist in the issues of an individual bank.

ILLUSTRATIONS

The reproduction of banknotes in the United Kingdom is governed by the Forgery and Counterfeiting Act 1981. Section 18 of the Act makes it an offence to reproduce without prior consent from the issuing authority any British currency note.

The Royal Bank of Scotland plc and its constituent banks are covered by the terms of the above Act. Those illustrated in this book are reproduced in reduced size and with the consent of the Bank. "Specimen Notes" are utilised where possible.

VALUATION

Attempts to place valuations on "collectables" are prone to be contentious, and in this respect banknotes are no exception. In a relatively new market prices take time to become stabilised and we have not yet reached the stage when we can emulate the traditional postage stamp catalogue. The writer would gladly have shirked the responsibility of including valuations in any form, but these are the very features on which both dealers and collectors place great store. If this book is to serve its purpose as a guide and source of information to its readers then some system of valuation must be incorporated. The system selected takes into account all relevant factors including known degrees of rarity. The price range quoted is that within which the collector may reasonably be expected to pay for the note in the grade of condition stated. It should be observed, however, that certain individual notes may possess features for which a dealer could with justification ask a premium.

Prices for Scottish notes. Supply and Demand are the ultimate factors in determining the value of a note offered for sale. A considerable quantity of Scottish material has been available on the market in recent years from sources now known to be exhausted, consequently when existing stocks are disposed of dealers face the possibility of experiencing difficulties in replacing them. On the other hand, demand can best be influenced by publicity and by the availability of information regarding a particular field and its scope. The publication of this book may act as a stimulant.

Perusal of dealers' lists and auction sales over the last few years reveals a degree of inconsistency in the prices of Scottish notes. In the writer's considered opinion a number are overpriced, but there are many other instances in which higher prices would be justified. The inconsistencies are often due to lack of knowledge of numbers available, and what might become available in the future. Release now of information regarding the actual numbers printed should enable a proper balance to be struck.

Important. It must be remembered that all issued notes listed in this book are redeemable at face value, either at the bank of issue or, in the case of banks no longer in existence, at the bank in which they are merged. Consequently the face value of a note forms an integral part of its valuation.

Grading. Grading terms similar to those used in numismatic circles are also employed to indicate the condition of banknotes.
These are:

UNC	Uncirculated	VF	Very fine
EF	Extremely fine	GF	Good fine
GVF	Good very fine	F	Fine

Two points are worthy of consideration. First, it has become clear that pre-1920 Scottish notes in the top grades (EF. and UNC.) are rarities, and as such justify the high prices asked by discerning dealers — much higher than the valuations shown in this book which refer to grade F. Secondly, the current design types, which have been with us for over 12 years, have largely been neglected by both dealers and collectors, resulting in the difficulty now of acquiring earlier dates and signature variations in uncirculated condition, and accounting for the expressions of surprise which will be occasioned while glancing at the price range quoted here for so-called current notes. Let it be stressed that these apply **only** to notes in a genuinely uncirculated condition. Lesser grades are still capable of being extracted from notes in circulation.

Valuation System. A simplified coding system in which price ranges are allied to a series of numbers 1 - 12 covering "under £ 10" to "over £ 1,000" with suitable price brackets in between, has been adopted. Two symbols X and Z are reserved for notes where surviving examples are yet to be recorded and for specimen and experimental notes unlikely to be made available to collectors. This system will permit easy up-dating, future price fluctuations being recorded by altering the price range and leaving the code numbers unchanged in the text, these being based on known scarcity. Thus, apart from new issues, this book can be kept up-to-date for many years.

The code numbers refer to "valuation" and not to "degrees of rarity." Rarity is of course a leading factor in determining a price, but visual attraction, historical importance and known availability have all been considered in selecting the appropriate valuation code number. In this the system differs from that employed in "Scottish Banknotes," which sought only to determine the known or estimated degree of rarity.

Gradings adopted for valuations

Notes issued before 1920	F/GF	Higher grades classified as scarce to rare.
Notes issued between 1920 - 45	VF/GVF	Higher grades generally available.
Notes issued between 1946 - 70	EF	Lower grades available at much lower prices.
Notes issued after 1970	UNC.	

These represent the grades generally available to collectors for any given period, and apart from certain rarities, should represent the minimum grade to be aimed at.

Valuation Code — 1986

Under £ 10	1
£ 10 - £ 20	2
£ 21 - £ 35	3
£ 36 - £ 50	4
£ 51 - £ 75	5
£ 76 - £ 100	6
£ 101 - £ 150	7
£ 151 - £ 200	8
£ 201 - £ 300	9
£ 301 - £ 500	10
£ 501 - £ 1000	11
Above £ 1000	12

X   No surviving issued note recorded.

Z   These notes unlikely to be available to collectors.

SCOTTISH BANKING IN THE 20th CENTURY

The continued progress of the Scottish banks during the present century is covered in detail in the standard work on the subject "Scottish Banking — a History 1695-1973" by Professor Checkland, so it need only be lightly touched on here. To the Collector the main feature is undoubtedly the series of mergers which resulted in the ten banks of issue which existed at the beginning of the century being reduced to the present figure of three.

In 1907 the Bank of Scotland purchased The Caledonian Banking Company Limited, founded at Inverness in 1838, and in the following year the Aberdeen-based North of Scotland Bank Limited and The Town & County Bank Limited merged. The first-mentioned union arose as a matter of financial expediency and the second was logical on geographical grounds. Neither merger upset the equilibrium of the system. For almost half a century thereafter, the remaining eight banks co-existed. They were in open competition with each other certainly, but the competition was on very conservative lines and somewhat muted. Each bank maintained a country-wide branch system, and each had its separate note issue, a factor which created a measure of confusion to visitors and tourists.

When in 1950 The Clydesdale Bank Limited with its main strength in the south-west and the North of Scotland Bank Limited, territorially dominant in the north-east, joined hands, there may have been some raising of eyebrows in the board rooms of the other banks, but the amalgamation could not be said to upset the proverbial apple cart. The situation was different, however, when in 1955 the Bank of Scotland and The Union Bank of Scotland Limited merged. These banks possessed a more or less equally distributed branch system, although administratively based in Edinburgh and Glasgow respectively. The computer age was about to dawn, and rationalisation offered a tempting advantage to larger institutions. The writing was on the wall, and further mergers were now inevitable.

The first of these took place when four years later The Commercial Bank of Scotland Limited, with the largest branch system in the country, joined forces with The National Bank of Scotland Limited to form National Commercial Bank of Scotland Limited and thus to create the country's largest bank. The next decade heralded a period of consolidation during which systems of computerisation and electronic accounting were pioneered. In these the Scottish banks led the field. In the post war years they had become much less highly committed, in terms of capital, to mechanised accounting than had their English counterparts, and a change-over to electronic methods entailed less scrapping of existing equipment. In 1969, the National Commercial and The Royal Bank, each with English subsidiaries, merged to form The National and Commercial Banking Group (now The Royal Bank of Scotland Banking Group). This was a holding company, the Scottish element becoming The Royal Bank of Scotland Limited (now The Royal Bank of Scotland plc) and that in England, Williams and Glyn's Bank plc. Almost immediately arrangements were entered into for the Bank of Scotland to absorb The British Linen Bank, and of the ten banks which greeted the advent of the 20th century, there remained but three. These three banks, however, embody all the resources of their constituents and by virtue of one of the unique features of Scottish banking law, also their combined note circulations, now totalling in excess of £ 500 million.

The various mergers are summarised as follows —

General Introduction

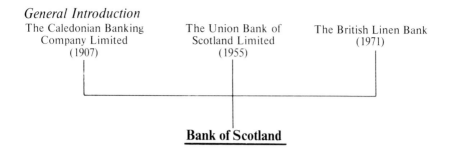

The Caledonian Banking
Company Limited
(1907)

The Union Bank of
Scotland Limited
(1955)

The British Linen Bank
(1971)

Bank of Scotland

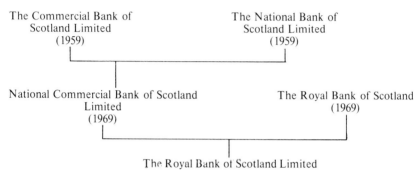

The Commercial Bank of
Scotland Limited
(1959)

The National Bank of
Scotland Limited
(1959)

National Commercial Bank of Scotland
Limited
(1969)

The Royal Bank of Scotland
(1969)

The Royal Bank of Scotland Limited

The Royal Bank of Scotland plc

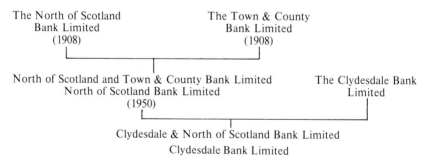

The North of Scotland
Bank Limited
(1908)

The Town & County
Bank Limited
(1908)

North of Scotland and Town & County Bank Limited
North of Scotland Bank Limited
(1950)

The Clydesdale Bank
Limited

Clydesdale & North of Scotland Bank Limited
Clydesdale Bank Limited

Clydesdale Bank PLC

Mergers in the 20th Century

Status of the Scottish Issues

The Introduction in "Scottish Banknotes" dealt with the history of the notes, and most British collectors of the series are well versed in the details of their unique story. It has become obvious, however, that this knowledge is not shared by many overseas collectors, and surprisingly enough by a number in England. Perusal of dealers' advertisements and of articles in numismatic journals reveals several misconceptions. The following paragraphs attempt to deal with some of these.

1. An apparent failure to appreciate the status and size of the Scottish note circulation, linking it with the small modern issues of the off-shore islands, the Isle of Man and the Channel Islands.

    Scotland has one of the oldest paper currencies in the world, the notes having circulated without interruption for almost 300 years. The average amount in circulation now exceeds one billion U.S.A. dollars, yes, $1,000,000,000!

2. There is a tendency abroad to refer to the notes as "Private Issues," occasionally coupled with the inference that they are at best "unauthorised" or at worst some kind of "funny money." The Scottish banks are sometimes referred to as "Private banks."

    Scottish notes are legal currency, authorised by Parliament and controlled by the Bank Charter Act of 1845 and by subsequent Acts. The banks are "Public banks," although some private banks did exist in Scotland until the early 19th century.

3. Resulting from various mergers, the number of banks of issue in Scotland have been reduced to three in number — there were ten at the beginning of the century. There is a tendency to regard the notes of former banks as "obsolete" or not redeemable. At recent auctions both in London and in U.S.A., some Scottish £ 100 notes were knocked down at well under their face value.

    Scottish notes are never invalidated. When one bank acquires another it assumes responsibility for its note issue. A Scottish bank regards a "promise to pay" to mean exactly what it says — no matter how long ago that promise was made.

UNCIRCULATED NOTES

Prior to 1950 it was the custom for tellers at Scottish banks to fold "new" £1 notes of Sizes A and B, and £5 notes of Size X into bundles of £20 and £100 respectively, before issuing them to the public. Genuinely uncirculated notes of these denominations will be found to have traces of a central fold. The large Size W notes were folded over twice, thus acquiring two fold traces. Such traces will tend to be present on all uncirculated notes of the period and should not be treated as a defect. Indeed, their presence will serve to confirm that the note in question has not been subjected to any cosmetic ironing treatment! After the early 1950s, all new notes were stored and issued by the tellers in a flat condition and uncirculated notes should be devoid of any fold traces. The old system did not die out overnight, however, and several tellers continued the practice of former generations.

"ARMS" and "EMBLEMS"

Reference in the text of this book to these terms may cause confusion, especially with overseas readers not versed in heraldry. "Arms" denote Coats of Arms as granted by the Lord Lyon King of Arms, supreme authority on heraldry in Scotland. He has extraordinary powers and wide-ranging penalties for misuse of Arms can be imposed by the Lyon Court. "Emblems" are merely distinguishing devices or designs aimed at providing institutions or companies with a form of visual identification easily recognised by the public. A good example of both terms can be found on the current note series of the Bank of Scotland where the Arms of the Bank are displayed on the front and where the Emblems of the three associated banks form part of the design on the back. Although on occasion derived from parts of the Arms, emblems do not require permission from the Lord Lyon.

THE
ROYAL BANK OF SCOTLAND plc

Sir Michael Herries, Chairman, The Royal Bank of Scotland Group plc,
and The Royal Bank of Scotland plc.

THE ROYAL BANK OF SCOTLAND plc

The Royal Bank of Scotland plc as it is now constituted is the result of the merger in 1969 of The Royal Bank of Scotland and the National Commercial Bank of Scotland Limited to form The Royal Bank of Scotland Limited. Much thought was given to this choice of title for the new Scottish bank. Combining the existing names was a time-honoured practice in such a merger, but this could result in something like "National Commercial and Royal Bank of Scotland Limited". Considerable prestige attached to the word "Royal" and retention of "Royal Bank of Scotland" as the title of the new bank made sense. The merged bank was an entirely new company however and as such could no longer shelter under the Charter granted to the old "Royal". It had therefore to register under the existing Companies Acts and in consequence was required to add "Limited" to its title. The merged bank and its English subsidiaries, Williams Deacons' Bank Limited, Glyn, Mills Co. and the National Bank Limited — were placed in the control of the National and Commercial Banking Group Limited formed for the purpose. The English Banks themselves merged in 1970 to form Williams and Glyn's Bank Limited. In 1979 the name of the Group was changed to The Royal Bank of Scotland Group Limited and in 1982 to conform with EEC Regulations, the word 'Limited' in the names of the Group and the two banks was replaced by 'plc'. In September 1985 the two Banks merged under the name The Royal Bank of Scotland plc with a branch system of some 900 branches operating throughout the country from the Shetland Islands to the Channel Islands.

In order to appreciate fully the standing of both the old Royal Bank of Scotland and the National Commercial Bank of Scotland Limited in the financial history of Scotland, it is essential to consider both separately, although in a book of this nature only a brief outline can be given.

The Royal Bank of Scotland plc
The Royal Bank of Scotland

Its origin can be indirectly traced to William Paterson's ill-fated attempt in the last years of the 17th century to found a Scottish trading colony at Darien on the Isthmus of Panama. As a result of the scheme's failure, Scotland was seriously impoverished and there was deep resentment at the hostility which in England had been shown to the enterprise. Some compensation for the Darien subscribers was forthcoming and the last Act of the Scottish Parliament before the 1707 Union directed that up to £ 232,884. 5s.0³/₄d should be paid to them in reimbursement of their losses. But by the Treaty of Union, England agreed to pay a sum of £ 398,065.10s to Scotland as an equivalent for the increased fiscal and other responsibilities which the country would have to bear and to compensate the Darien subscribers. Settlement of the Equivalent was largely by way of debentures and in 1724 the holders of the debentures were incorporated by Act of Parliament as the Equivalent Company. A Royal Charter was granted in 1727 to those of its members who elected to transfer their stock to become incorporated in The Royal Bank of Scotland. The Royal Bank quickly took advantage of the right which all banks had under the Common Law of Scotland to issue notes, the first being dated 8th December 1727.

The expansion of the Bank from those modest beginnings can be divided into three distinct phases. The first of some 100 years, was spent in building up its business in Edinburgh and Glasgow. The second phase again lasted nearly 100 years — from 1833 to 1930 during which the Bank followed the general policy of the time by founding new branches and amalgamating with other banks. In 1864 the business of the Dundee Banking Company was acquired. Drummond's Bank in London was acquired in 1924 and the business of the Western Branch of the Bank of England was taken over in 1930. The third phase from 1930 onwards saw the acquisition of Williams Deacons Bank Limited in that year and of Glyn Mills and Co. in 1939. In this phase, though expansion was continued, the method was different; the three banks, the Three Banks Group, as it was known, continued their business as separate entities.

The National Commercial Bank of Scotland Limited

The Bank was formed in 1959 by the merger of the Commercial Bank of Scotland Limited and the National Bank of Scotland Limited, two old-established Banks. The Commercial Bank of Scotland opened for business in Edinburgh in 1810 as the Commercial Banking Company of

The Royal Bank of Scotland plc

Scotland and was promoted essentially by businessmen to be independent of private bankers who, to some extent, at that time dominated the then three existing chartered banks. It was given a Royal Charter in 1831 and justified its national aspirations by embarking on a branch system which in its day became the largest in Scotland. Two small banks were absorbed, the Caithness Bank in 1825 and the Arbroath Banking Company in 1844. In 1954 the Commercial was the first British bank to absorb a hire-purchase company, the Scottish Midland Guarantee Trust. In 1966 under a Scheme of arrangement, the English branches of the National Bank Limited which operated largely in Ireland, were taken over and formed into a wholly-owned subsidiary.

The note issue of the Commercial Bank is of great interest to collectors as not only were changes in design numerous, but many of the designs were outstanding in their technical and artistic qualities.

The National Bank of Scotland was established in Edinburgh in 1825 and from its inception it adopted a policy of branch expansion throughout the country. In 1831 it, too, was granted a Royal Charter and in 1864 was the first of the Scottish Banks to open in London. The Commercial Banking Company of Aberdeen was absorbed in 1833 and the Perth Union Bank in 1836.

In 1918 an offer by Lloyds Bank Limited to purchase the capital was accepted, the National Bank of Scotland Limited continuing to operate under its own name. The English bank's interest, however, was pared down to approximately 36.6 per cent in 1959 when the National joined with the Commercial.

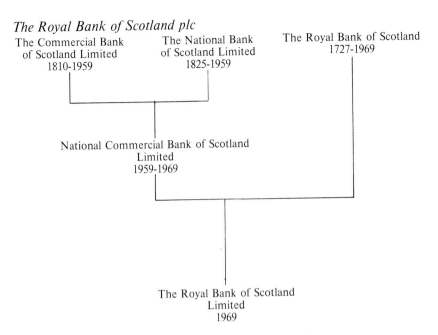

The Royal Bank of Scotland plc

The Commercial Bank of Scotland Limited 1810-1959

The National Bank of Scotland Limited 1825-1959

The Royal Bank of Scotland 1727-1969

National Commercial Bank of Scotland Limited 1959-1969

The Royal Bank of Scotland Limited 1969

The Royal Bank of Scotland plc

1982

Acquisitions by the above banks:

The Commercial Bank of Scotland Limited

1825. The Caithness Banking Company
1844. The Arbroath Banking Company

The National Bank of Scotland Limited

1833. The Aberdeen Commercial Banking Company
1836. The Perth Union Bank

The Royal Bank of Scotland

1864. The Dundee Banking Company
1924. Drummonds Bank
1930. Williams Deacons Bank Limited
1939. Glyn Mills and Co.

Banknotes of note issuing banks listed above are still redeemable at The Royal Bank of Scotland plc — but of course their value as collectors' items is likely to be much greater than their face value.

The Note Issues

If the foregoing account of the merger gives rise to any confusion, need we deal with the note issues of the old and the new Royal Banks on the basis that they are two separate institutions? Would it not be more simple for our purpose to consider the present bank as an extension of its former namesake and list the notes accordingly? Certainly it has been the Bank's own policy in recent years to project its public image in a manner which suggests that degree of continuity. After all there has been a Royal Bank operating in Scotland since 1727 and surely it would be more expedient to deal with the note issues as if the events of 1969 had never taken place? Erudite collectors however have never been prone to sacrifice historical accuracy upon the altar of expediency. Banknote collectors are no exception and they will continue to regard the year 1969 as that of the demise of the old Royal Bank, and the birth of the new. What happened in that year was a true merger and not a takeover and it spelled the end of the road for the note issues of both National Commercial and the old Royal. The catalogue commences therefore with the first issue of notes by the new and merged bank.

1. INSCRIBED

"THE ROYAL BANK OF SCOTLAND LIMITED"

The First or "Interim Series"

Perhaps this could more appropriately be termed the "Forth Bridge Series" but as such it could be confused with the issues of the former National Commercial Bank. It is safer therefore to label it the "Interim Series", for indeed that is what it was. The five denominations were designed and engraved by Bradbury Wilkinson and Company Ltd. to reflect in as equal a manner as possible the principal features on the notes of the two merging banks, and the designs are briefly as follows:—
One Pound. The "Bridge" motif of the National Commercial is retained as the main design but it is the new Road Bridge over the Forth Estuary which now has pride of place, the older Rail Bridge being relegated to the background. The watermark consists of the profile head of David Dale, adapted from that shown on the last £1 and £5 notes of the Royal Bank. The back illustrates the Coat of Arms of the former Royal Bank and now adopted as that of the merged bank. Green and multicolour.
Five Pounds. The front design bears a strong resemblance to that of the final Royal note of this denomination, but the back design is similar to that on the last National Commercial £5 note illustrating Edinburgh Castle. Blue and multicolour.

Ten Pounds. The design is very similar to that of the National Commercial with the back illustrating the Tay Road Bridge and the town of Dundee. This denomination was not represented in the last Royal series. Brown and multicolour.

Twenty and One Hundred Pounds. These have the Arms featured on the front design with the portrait of the Right Honourable Alexander Henderson of Press, which appeared as a watermark on the 1957 series of The National Bank of Scotland notes. The back design consists of an illustration of the Forth Road Bridge. The Twenty pound note is purple and multicolour and the hundred pound note is red and multicolour.

Each denomination bears the signatures of the two General Managers, John B. Burke (formerly National Commercial) and A. P. Robertson (formerly Royal). As a nice display of impartiality the order in which the signatures appear alternates with each denomination. The notes are in the now standardised colours, the One Pound and Five Pound notes being encoded for electronic sorting. All denominations incorporate the metallic strip and the printers' imprint is on the back.

Although the life of the Interim Series was relatively short it still managed to produce a variation on two of its denominations. In 1970 A. P. Robertson retired and John B. Burke became the sole senior executive officer under the title of Managing Director, the first use of this designation among the Scottish banks. To accommodate the change, the bottom margin of the One Pound note was suitably modified, but no modification was necessary on the Five Pound note apart from the single signature and the designation Managing Director.

On the introduction of the new notes, those of the two merging banks were gradually withdrawn from circulation, but of course their validity continues.

One Pound. Size D. Green and multicolour. Encoded. With printed signatures of A. P. Robertson and J. B. Burke, General Managers.

					EF
1.	1-1	19 Mar 1969	A/1 to A/45	1,000,000 each serial	1
	1-2	19 Mar 1969 SPECIMEN A/1 000000	A/1 Overprinted in red. Two punch holes.	100	Z

The Royal Bank of Scotland Limited

One Pound. As above but with one signature only — that of J. B. Burke, now designated Managing Director.

					EF
6.	6-1	15 Jul 1970	A/46 to A/67	1,000,000 each	1
			A/68	200,000	1
	6-2	15 Jul 1970 SPECIMEN A/46 000000	A/46 Overprinted in red. Two punch holes.	100	Z

Five Pounds. Size Z. Blue and multicolour. Encoded. With printed signatures of J. B. Burke and A. P. Robertson, General Managers.

					EF
2.	2-1	19 Mar 1969	A/1 to A/14	1,000,000 each	2
	2-2	19 Mar 1969 SPECIMEN A/1 000000	A/1 Overprinted in red. Two punch holes.	100	Z

J. B. Burke
General Manager and Managing Director, Royal Bank of Scotland Limited 1969-82, and Deputy Chairman of the Royal Bank Group 1982-84.

A. P. Robertson
Deputy General Manager, Royal Bank of Scotland 1966-69, and General Manager Royal Bank of Scotland Limited 1969-70.

The Royal Bank of Scotland Limited

Five Pounds. As above but with one signature only – that of J. B. Burke, Managing Director.

					EF
7.	7-1	15 Jul 1970	A/15 to A/19	1,000,000 each	2
	7-2	15 Jul 1970 A/15 000000	A/15 Overprinted in red. Two punch holes.	100	Z

Ten Pounds. Size Y. Brown and multicolour. With printed signatures of A. P. Robertson and J. B. Burke, General Managers.

					GVF
3.	3-1	19 Mar 1969	A/1	500,000	4
	3-2	19 Mar 1969 SPECIMEN A/1 000000	A/1 Overprinted in red. Two punch holes.	100	Z

Twenty Pound. Size X. Purple and multicolour. With printed signatures of J. B. Burke and A. P. Robertson, General Managers.

					GVF
4.	4-1	19 Mar 1969	A/1	500,000	4
	4-2	19 Mar 1969 SPECIMEN A/1 000000	A/1 Overprinted in red. Two punch holes.	100	Z

One Hundred Pounds. Size X. Red and multicolour. With printed signatures of A. P. Robertson and J. B. Burke, General Managers.

					GVF
5.	5-1	19 Mar 1969	A/1	30,000	8
	5-2	19 Mar 1969 SPECIMEN A/1 000000	A/1 Overprinted in black. Two punch holes.	100	Z

The Royal Bank of Scotland Limited
The Castle Series

During the currency of the "Interim Series" much thought was given to the provision of entirely new designs. The "Bridge" motif had enjoyed a long life, having graced the notes of three banks, the National, the National Commercial and latterly the new Royal, but a change was now due. The distinctive emblem or "logo" of the Bank and of Williams and Glyns was already becoming familiar to the public both north and south of the Border but nowhere did it appear on the Royal Bank notes. Bradbury Wilkinson and Company Limited were accordingly instructed to design a new series incorporating a Scottish theme and including the appropriate emblem of The Group. As a result there emerged the issue best referred to as the "Castle Series".

As a consequence of its turbulent history, Scotland has many castles and it was decided that illustrations of certain of these would provide a suitable theme for the designs of the new series. Many of the castles are well known and to restrict the selection to the five required for the series was no easy task. Some of the more famous are now in ruin, but a ruined building, no matter how artistically portrayed or how romantic its appeal, might be regarded as inappropriate in the design for notes of a Scottish bank traditionally renowned for its strength and stability. With the field thus narrowed to castles still in habitation and in addition capable of being boldly portrayed, the final selection consisted of the castles listed overleaf.

Although castles were to provide the main theme for the new series it was decided to illustrate them on the back of the notes thus enabling the artist and engraver to present them to advantage without interference from the essential wording. Consequently the notes all bear a similar front design consisting of the Arms of the Bank in an oval panel, balanced by a similar panel containing in watermark form, a portrait of Adam Smith, the noted Scottish economist and author of the standard work "The Wealth of Nations". As in the previous issue, the One Pound and Five Pound notes are encoded and all denominations possess the customary metal band.

1-2
(p. 21)

1-2R
(p. 21)

6-2
(p. 22)

2-2
(p. 22)

2-2R
(p. 22)

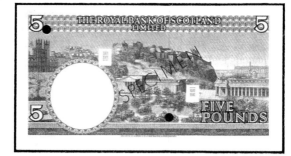

7-2
(p. 23)

3-2
(p. 23)

3-2R
(p. 23)

4-2
(p. 23)

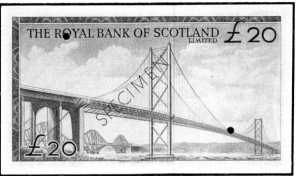

4-2R
(p. 23)

5-2
(p. 23)

5-2R
(p. 23)

8-2
(p. 34)

8-2R
(p. 34)

9-2
(p. 35)

9-2R
(p. 35)

10-2
(p. 36)

10-2R
(p. 36)

11-2
(p. 36)

11-2R
(p. 36)

12-2
(p. 37)

12-2R
(p. 37)

13-2
(p. 39)

13-2R
(p. 39)

14-2
(p. 39)

14-2R
(p. 39)

15-2
(p. 40)

15-2R
(p. 40)

16-2
(p. 40)

16-2R
(p. 40)

17-2
(p. 40)

17-2R
(p. 40)

The five castles illustrated are:

£1 Note

Edinburgh Castle. The Castle Rock, rising some 200 feet above Princes Street, has been a fortification since prehistoric times. The Castle itself is steeped in antiquity and since the 11th century has been closely linked with the history of Scotland. It also provided the main feature on the early notes of The Commercial Bank of Scotland.

£5 Note

Culzean Castle (pronounced "Cullain"). Situated on a cliff on the Ayrshire coast some eleven miles south of Ayr, it was formerly the seat of the Marquis of Ailsa. It is now one of the properties of the National Trust for Scotland and a well-known tourist attraction.

£10 Note

Glamis Castle. The County of Angus was reputedly the scene of the murder of King Malcolm II of Scotland in 1031. It is the seat of the Earl of Strathmore.

£20 Note

Brodick Castle. The Isle of Arran was formerly held by the Dukes of Montrose. Now administered by the National Trust for Scotland.

£100 Note

Balmoral Castle. A Royal residence in Deeside and was built in 1853 to replace an existing building. It was a great favourite of Queen Victoria and has provided successive Royal Families with a suitable location in which to enjoy periods of rest, relaxation, and above all, privacy. Balmoral Castle was also illustrated on the back of the One Pound notes of the Town and County Bank in 1860s.

The Royal Bank of Scotland Limited
One Pound. Size D. Green and Multicolour. Encoded. Printed signature of J. B. Burke, Managing Director.

					EF
8.	8-1	5 Jan 1972	A/1 to A/45	1,000,000 each	2
		2 Apr 1973	A/46 to A/67	1,000,000 each	1
		1 Mar 1974	A/68 to A/77	1,000,000 each	1
		1 May 1975	A/78 to A/99 B/1 to B/3	1,000,000 each	1
		3 May 1976	B/4 to B/18	1,000,000 each	1
		3 May 1977	B/19 to B/38	1,000,000 each	1
		2 May 1978	B/39 to B/60	1,000,000 each	1
		1 May 1979	B/61 to B/80	1,000,000 each	1
		1 May 1980	B/81 to B/99 C/1 to C/7	1,000,000 each	1
		10 Jan 1981	C/8 to C/32	1,000,000 each	1
		1 May 1981	C/33 to C/57	1,000,000 each	1
	8-2	5 Jan 1972 SPECIMEN A/1 000000	A/1 Overprinted in black as all subsequent specimen notes.	100	Z

Five Pounds. Size Z. Blue and multicolour. Encoded. Printed signature of J. B. Burke, Managing Director.

					EF
9.	9-1	5 Jan 1972	A/1 to A/10	1,000,000 each	3
		2 Apr 1973	A/11 to A/18	1,000,000 each	2
		1 Mar 1974	A/19 to A/27	1,000,000 each	2
		1 May 1975	A/28 to A/37	1,000,000 each	2
		3 May 1976	A/38 to A/49	1,000,000 each	2
		3 May 1977	A/50 to A/55	1,000,000 each	2
		2 May 1978	A/56 to A/61	1,000,000 each	2

The Royal Bank of Scotland Limited

				EF
1 May 1979	A/62 to A/73	1,000,000 each	2
1 May 1980	A/74 to A/89	1,000,000 each	2
10 Jan 1981	A/90 to A/99 B/1 to B/2	1,000,000 each	2
1 May 1981	B/3 to B/12	1,000,000 each	2
	B/13	400,000	2
9-2	5 Jan 1972 SPECIMEN A/1 00000	A/1	100	Z

Ten Pounds. Size Y. Brown and multicolour. Printed signature of J. B. Burke, Managing Director.

The rapid growth in the popularity of this denomination is interesting. Early printings were on a relatively small scale, based on previous requirements. During the ten year lifetime of the National Commercial Bank for instance, a total of 500,000 notes had proved to be sufficient and requirements for the first two years of the Castle Series were fixed at that figure. Inflation however caused a marked change in public readiness to come to terms with this hitherto unpopular denomination and demand for it was suddenly stepped up. The numbers printed for each date suggests that estimated requirements were constantly short of actual demand. When Cash Dispensers were installed on a country-wide basis in the late 1970s requirements for the Ten Pound note suddenly rocketed. In the year 1981 a total printing of 23,000,000 notes became necessary.

					EF
10	10-1	5 Jan 1972	A/1	500,000	4
		1 Mar 1974	A/1 & A/2	500,000 each	3
		1 May 1975	A/2	500,000	3
			A/3	820,000	3
		15 Dec 1975	A/3	180,000	3
			A/4 to A/6	1,000,000 each	3
			A/7	700,000	3
		3 May 1976	A/7	300,000	3
			A/8	1,000,000	3
			A/9	200,000	3
		3 May 1977	A/9	800,000	3
			A/10 & A/11	1,000,000 each	3

					EF
			A/12	200,000	3
10.	10-1	2 May 1978	A/12	800,000	3
			A/13 to A/15	1,000,000 each	3
			A/16	700,000	3
		1 May 1979	A/16	300,000	3
			A/17 to A/22	1,000,000 each	3
			A/23	200,000	3
		1 May 1980	A/23	800,000	3
			A/24 to A/27	1,000,000 each	3
			A/28	200,000	3
		10 Jan 1981	A/28	800,000	3
			A/29 to A/32	1,000,000 each	3
			A/33	200,000	3
		1 May 1981	A/33	800,000	3
			A/34 to A/38	1,000,000 each	3
			A/39	200,000	3
		1 Dec 1981	A/39	800,000	3
			A/40 to A/48	1,000,000 each	3
			A/49	200,000	3
	10-2	5 Jan 1972 SPECIMEN A/1 000000	A/1	100	Z

Twenty Pounds. Size X. Purple and mulitcolour. Printed signature of J. B. Burke, Managing Director.

					EF
11.	11-1	5 Jan 1972	A/1	500,000	5
		3 May 1977	A/1	500,000	4
		1 May 1979	A/2	500,000	4
		1 May 1980	A/2	300,000	4
		10 Jan 1981	A/2	700,000	4
			A/3	800,000	4
		1 May 1981	A/3	200,000	4
			A/4	1,000,000	3
			A/5	1,000,000	3
			A/6	50,000	4
	11-2	5 Jan 1972 SPECIMEN A/1 000000	A/1	100	Z

One Hundred Pounds. Size X. Red and multicolour. Printed signature of J. B. Burke, Managing Director.

					GVF
12.	12-1	5 Jan 1972	A/1	30,000	9
		1 May 1975	A/1	30,000	8
		3 May 1977	A/1	40,000	8
		1 May 1979	A/1	20,000	8
		1 May 1980	A/1	40,000	8
		1 May 1981	A/1	60,000	8
	12-2	5 Jan 1972	A/1	100	Z
		SPECIMEN			
		A/1 000000			

2. INSCRIBED
"THE ROYAL BANK OF SCOTLAND plc"

Together with all public limited companies already registered under previous Companies Acts the Bank was required to re-register, altering the title from The Royal Bank of Scotland Limited to The Royal Bank of Scotland plc in 1982. This had no effect on the operation of the Bank but of course entailed a change in the title on the note issue.

The change also coincided with an alteration in the printed signature. John B. Burke, whose signature has been familiar to collectors from the days of the final issue of National Commercial Bank was appointed Deputy Chairman of the Royal Bank Group and Charles R. Winter was appointed to succeed him as Managing Director, his signature in that capacity appearing on the new "plc" notes.

Apart from the changes in title and signature the design of the notes is otherwise identical to that of the former "Limited" issue, and they continue to utilise the existing system of serial numbering. However, the imprint on the reverse side now simply reads "Bradbury Wilkinson".

Encoding. In June 1983 it was decided to dispense with encoding symbols on the £1 and £5 notes, as the Crosfield sorting machines were no longer used by the Scottish banks.

Charles M. Winter, Managing Director 1982-1985,
Chief Executive 1985-   , The Royal Bank of Scotland plc.

One Pound. Size D. Green and multicolour. Encoded. Printed signature of Charles R. Winter, Managing Director.

					EF
13.	13-1	3 May 1982	C/58 to C/66	1,000,000 each	1
	13-2	3 May 1982 SPECIMEN C/58 000000	C/58	100	Z

Notes no longer encoded

					EF
13.	13-3	1 Oct 1983	C/67 to C/81	1,000,000 each	1
		4 Jan 1984	C/82 to C/99	1,000,000 each	1
			D/1 to D/7	1,000,000	1
		3 Jan 1985	D/8 to D/32	1,000,000	1
		No SPECIMEN notes were printed for these dates.			

Five Pounds. Size Z. Blue and multicolour. Encoded. Printed signature of Charles R. Winter, Managing Director.

					EF
14.	14-1	3 May 1982	B/13 B/14 to B/24	600,000 1,000,000 each	2 2
		5 Jan 1983	B/25 to B/36	1,000,000 each	2
	14-2	3 May 1982 SPECIMEN B/13 000000	B/13	100	Z

Notes no longer encoded

					EF
14.	14-3	4 Jan 1984	B/37 to B/44	1,000,000 each	2
		3 Jan 1985	B/45 to B/58	1,000,000 each	2
		No SPECIMEN notes were printed for these dates			

The Royal Bank of Scotland plc
Ten Pounds. Size Y. Brown and multicolour. Printed signature of
Charles R. Winter, Managing Director.

					EF
15.	15-1	3 May 1982	A/49	800,000	3
			A/50 to A/56	1,000,000 each	3
			A/57	200,000	3
		5 Jan 1983	A/57	800,000	3
			A/58 to A/65	1,000,000 each	3
			A/66	200,000	3
		4 Jan 1984	A/66	800,000	3
			A/67 to A/76	1,000,000 each	3
			A/76	200,000	3
		3 Jan 1985	A/76	800,000	3
			A/77 to A/88	1,000,000 each	3
	15-2	3 May 1982 SPECIMEN A/49 000000	A/49	100	Z

Twenty Pounds. Size X. Purple and multicolour. Printed signature of
Charles R. Winter, Managing Director.

					EF
16.	16-1	3 May 1982	A/6	950,000	3
			A/7	1,000,000	3
			A/8	50,000	4
	16-2	3 May 1982 SPECIMEN A/6 000000	A/6	100	Z

One Hundred Pounds. Size X. Red and multicolour. Printed signature of
Charles R. Winter, Managing Director.

					EF
17.	17-1	3 May 1982	A/1	50,000	8
		3 Jan 1985	A/1	100,000	8
	17-2	3 May 1982 SPECIMEN A/1 000000	A/1	100	Z

THE COMMERCIAL BANK OF SCOTLAND LIMITED 1810-1959

The Commercial Bank of Scotland Limited, 14 George Street, Edinburgh.
In 1847 the Commercial Bank having commissioned architect David Rhind of Edinburgh to build a new bank on the site previously occupied by the Royal College of Physicians, transferred their business to 14 George Street from the 142 High Street Office. This continued to be the Head Office of the Commercial Bank up to the merger with the National Bank in 1959. It is now the Edinburgh, George Street Office of the Royal Bank of Scotland plc and in addition houses an Overseas Branch of the Bank.

41

THE COMMERCIAL BANK OF SCOTLAND LIMITED
Founded 1810

Together with The National Bank of Scotland Limited formed National Commercial Bank of Scotland Limited in 1959.

All notes are still valid and payable by The Royal Bank of Scotland plc.

The expansion which marked the earlier history of this bank continued in the present century until in 1959, when its separate identity came to an end, it had the largest branch system in the country and also the largest note circulation amounting to £ 20 million. It was the first British bank to absorb a hire purchase company (now more appropriately termed a Finance Company). This action drew murmurs of disapproval and expressions of incredulity from the ultra conservative banking circles of the periods, but as soon as the implications had been digested, every bank in the United Kingdom joined in a mad scramble to follow the example.

Set Numbers

A distinctive feature of Commercial Bank notes is the allocation of "Set" numbers. This expedient was introduced for accounting and record purposes and the "sets" do not always correspond to individual design series, sometimes as many as four set numbers existing for one basic design type. However, as the set number is always used in conjunction with the serial letter in numbering the notes, they are a useful guide to collectors in distinguishing the various issues and also the variations within these issues. Each denomination had separate set numbers.

The First Bradbury Wilkinson Series

For many years Commercial Bank notes had been printed by Perkins Bacon and Company, but in 1886 it was decided to award the contract to Bradbury Wilkinson and Company and an entirely new series was designed. As this series continued in issue well into the twentieth century it seems appropriate to commence our listing in that year.

The main feature of the new design was borrowed from that in the previous series and consists of the figures sculptured on the pediment of the Head Office building. The notes themselves are well − even elaborately − designed but the overall effect is somewhat less attractive than some of the other "Commercial" issues. This is perhaps due to the fact that the colour combination, a buff overlay on the dull blue tint of the basic plate, results in a rather flat appearance in the general design. The probable reason for the apparent lack of contrast was to make the task of forgery by photographic methods more difficult, and contemporary security printers had suddenly become alerted to the inherent dangers of photography. The notes for the 1885 series of the Bank of Scotland, printed in inks devised by Professor Crum Brown of Edinburgh University, are evidence of a similar approach to the problem.

Numerically this was a large issue covering a period of twenty years. Unfortunately however there are now relatively few survivors. The series reflects the growing increase in the circulation of Scottish notes, particularly of the One Pound denomination. It should be remembered that one pound notes had become something of a Scottish tradition, this denomination having been prohibited in England since 1825. The convenience, portability and reliability of the notes appealed to the Scottish public which preferred them to the current gold sovereigns. At the time of writing the unpopularity of the new one pound coin as a replacement for the Bank of England note of that denomination illustrates the point, although the public south of the Border will no doubt eventually come to terms with the coin. In contrast however the ten pound note was no longer proving popular in Scotland and this denomination was omitted from the new series and formed no part of any future issue of the Commercial Bank. Its popularity revived suddenly around 1970 but by that time the "Commercial" had retired from the ranks of the Scottish banks of Issue.

The old custom of having the notes bound into books by the printers prior to supply to the Bank survived to this series, the one pound notes being bound into books of 500 notes and the higher denominations into books of 200.

The Commercial Bank of Scotland Limited
One Pound. Designed, engraved and printed by Bradbury Wilkinson and Co. Ltd. Blue with buff overlay, back printed in a bright shade of green. No watermark. Size A. Sets 14, 15, 16 and 17. Hand-signed on behalf of the Accountant and the Cashier, but from Set 15 the Accountant's signature is in printed form. Supplied to the Bank bound in books of 500 notes.

Printers' imprint "Bradbury Wilkinson & Co." The £ 1 specimen note for 1 July 1886 illustrated in the colour plates is a unique Bradbury Wilkinson archive specimen numbered to indicate the actual printing order of 14/A 1/1 to 14/A 200/500 i.e. the 500th note in the 200th book.

Set 14.

					F
36a	36a-1	1 July 1886	14/A	100,000	10
		3 Jan 1887	14/B 14/C	100,000 each	10
			14/D	50,000	10
		3 Jan 1888	14/D	50,000	10
			14/E 14/F 14/G	100,000 each	10
		3 Jan 1889	14/H 14/I 14/J	100,000 each	10
		3 Jan 1890	14/K 14/L 14/M	100,000 each	10
		3 Jan 1891	14/N 14/O	100,000 each	10
		2 Jan 1892	14/P 14/Q	100,000 each	10
			14/R	50,000	10
	36a-2	SPECIMEN 1 July 1886	14/A	20	Z
		SPECIMEN 3 Jan 1887 (red)	14/B	20	Z

Set 15. Printers' imprint "Bradbury Wilkinson and Co. Ltd". Printed signature of the Accountant and hand-signed on behalf of the Cashier.

					F
36b	36b-1	2 Jan 1892	15/A	100,000	10
		2 Jan 1893	15/B 15/C	100,000 each	10
		2 Jan 1894	15/D 15/E 15/F 15/G	100,000 each	10
		2 Jan 1895	15/H 15/J 15/K	100,000 each	10
		2 Jan 1896	15/L 15/M 15/N 15/O	100,000 each	10
		2 Jan 1897	15/P 15/Q 15/R 15/S 15/T	100,000 each	10
		3 Jan 1898	15/U 15/V 15/W 15/X 15/Y	100,000 each	10
		3 Jan 1899	15/Z	100,000	10

Set 16. Similar to previous Set, but serial numbers in red.

					F
36b	36b-1	3 Jan 1899	16/A 16/B 16/C	100,000 each	10
		3 Jan 1900	16/D 16/E 16/F 16/G	100,000 each	10
		3 Jan 1901	16/H 16/I 16/J 16/K	100,000 each	10
		3 Jan 1902	16/L 16/M	100,000 each	10
			16/N	25,000	10

Set 17. Similar to Set 15.

					F
36b	36b-1	3 Jan 1903	17/A 17/B 17/C	100,000 each	10
		4 Jan 1904	17/E 17/F 17/G	100,000 each	10
		4 Jan 1905	17/H 17/I 17/J	100,000 each	10
		4 Jan 1906	17/K 17/L 17/M 17/N 17/O 17/P 17/Q	100,000 each	10
	36b-2	4 Jan 1904 SPECIMEN	17/E	20	Z

The Commercial Bank of Scotland Limited
Five Pounds. Set 12. Size W. Blue with buff overlay. Back printed in brown. Hand-signed on behalf of the Accountant and the Manager. Printed in books of 200 notes.

					F
37	37-1	3 Jan 1887	12/A	10,000	11
		3 Jan 1888	12/A	16,000	11
		3 Jan 1889	12/A	10,000	11
		3 Jan 1890	12/A	4,000	11
		3 Jan 1890	12/B	6,000	11
		3 Jan 1891	12/B	20,000	11
		2 Jan 1893	12/B	14,000	11
		3 Jan 1894	12/C	10,000	11
		3 Jan 1895	12/C	10,000	11
		3 Jan 1896	12/C	20,000	11
		3 Jan 1898	12/D	10,000	11
		3 Jan 1899	12/D	10,000	11
		3 Jan 1900	12/D	10,000	11
		3 Jan 1901	12/D	10,000	11
		3 Jan 1902	12/E	5,000	11
		3 Jan 1903	12/E	5,000	11
		4 Jan 1904	12/E	15,000	11
		4 Jan 1905	12/E	20,000	11
		2 Jan 1906	12/F	14,000	11
	37-2	3 Jan 1887 SPECIMEN	A	20	Z

Twenty Pounds. Set 10. Size W. Blue with buff overlay. Back printed in brown. Hand-signed on behalf of the Accountant and the Manager. Printed in books of 200 notes.

					F
38	38-1	3 Jan 1887	10/A	5,000	X
		3 Jan 1895	10/A	4,000	X
		3 Jan 1896	10/A	8,000	X
		3 Jan 1898	10/A	3,000	X

The Commercial Bank of Scotland Limited
Set 10. Similar to previous Set.

					F
38	38-1	3 Jan 1899	10/B	2,000	X
		3 Jan 1902	10/B	2,000	X
		3 Jan 1903	10/B	4,000	X
		4 Jan 1904	10/B	3,000	X
		4 Jan 1905	10/B	3,000	X
		4 Jan 1906	10/B	5,000	X
	38-2	SPECIMEN 3 Jan 1887 red	A	20	Z

One Hundred Pounds. Set 9. Size W. Blue with buff overlay. Back printed in brown. Hand-signed. Printed in books of 200 notes.

					F
39	39-1	3 Jan 1887	9/A	4,000	X
		3 Jan 1889	9/A	1,000	X
		3 Jan 1890	9/A	1,000	X
		3 Jan 1891	9/A	1,000	X
		2 Jan 1892	9/A	1,000	X
		2 Jan 1894	9/A	1,000	X
		2 Jan 1895	9/A	1,000	X
		2 Jan 1896	9/A	1,000	X
		3 Jan 1898	9/A	1,000	X
		3 Jan 1900	9/A	1,000	X
		3 Jan 1902	9/A	1,000	X
		3 Jan 1903	9/A	1,000	X
		4 Jan 1905	9/A	1,000	X
		4 Jan 1906	9/A	1,000	X
		2 Jan 1907	9/A	600	X
	39-2	3 Jan 1887 SPECIMEN	9/A	20	Z

The first Bradbury Wilkinson Series had been in issue for some twenty years. In a historical sense it had spanned the period from Queen Victoria's Golden Jubilee, through the Boer War, and well into the reign of Edward VII.

The Commercial Bank of Scotland Limited
The total numbers of notes issued were:—

£ 1	7,175,000
£ 5	219,000
£ 20	36,500
£ 100	17,600

Twenty Specimen Notes were provided for each denomination. When compared with current Scottish issues these figures seem almost insignificant. It is unlikely that any of the £ 100 notes have survived — at least none appears to have been recorded. One hundred pounds in these days represented a large sum of money, more in fact than the annual salary of many of the Bank's own employees. Who would be tempted to lay aside a note representing such a fortune merely as a souvenir? The existence of survivors of the £ 20 denomination is also doubtful but it is just possible that one or two have been "salted away" somewhere to emerge eventually and delight some collector. Examples of the two lower denominations are known, but they are scarce.

A new series was now considered by the Bank, and it is indicative of the good relationship existing between it and the printers that Bradbury Wilkinson were again approached on the matter. This new series was introduced in 1907.

The Second Bradbury Wilkinson Series

Once again the Head Office building features in the new designs, but now is transferred from the back of the notes to the upper part of the frontal design. Here it is joined by two other principal offices of the Bank. On the left we have the chief office in Glasgow (Gordon Street) and on the right that in London (Lombard Street). Perhaps the intention was for the Edinburgh-based bank to emphasise its country-wide representation. Indeed this aspect of its policy was soon to be expanded to the extent that by the advent of World War II the "Commercial" had the largest branch system of all the Scottish banks.

The back design consists of the Bank's emblem, devised from its Seal, contained within a complex pattern of white-line engraving. The emblem contains the motto "Ditat Servata Fides" (Keep Faith and Prosper).

The new series comprises two distinct issues which are now to be dealt with separately.

The First Issue

In this the basic engraved plate was printed in black, with lithographic overlays in yellow, orange and blue. The overall effect of this colour combination is bold and attractive. This issue was short-lived being replaced by the Second Issue, which will be dealt with later, and embraces some of the scarcest of all 20th century Scottish notes. In fact, survivors of the £ 20 and £ 100 denominations have yet to be recorded by the writer, and only a few of the One Pound notes and a solitary example of the Five Pound note are known. Twenty Specimen notes, without serial number and perforated "Specimen" were provided for each denomination. A complete set of these is held in the collection of the Institute of Bankers in Scotland.

⌐1907-1908

One Pound. Set 18. Size A. Black. Printed signature of L. M. Mackay, Accountant, and hand-signed on behalf of the Cashier.

					F
40.	40-1	2 Jan 1907	18/A	100,000	11
		2 Jan 1908	18/B 18/C 18/D 18/E	100,000 each	11
	40-2	2 Jan 1908 SPECIMEN	—	20	Z

Five Pounds. Set 13. Size W. Black. Hand-signed on behalf of the Accountant and the Manager.

					F
.41.	41-1	2 Jan 1908	13/A	18,800	12
	41-2	2 Jan 1908 SPECIMEN	—	20	Z

Twenty Pounds. Set 11. Size W. Black. Hand-signed on behalf of the Accountant and the Manager.

					F
42.	42-1	2 Jan 1907	11/A	3,000	X
	42-2	2 Jan 1907 SPECIMEN	—	20	Z

One Hundred Pounds. Set 10. Size W. Black. Hand-signed by the Accountant and the Manager, or on their behalf.

					F
43.	43-1	2 Jan 1907	10/A	600	X
	43-2	2 Jan 1907 SPECIMEN	—	20	Z

Illustrations featured on the Second Bradbury Wilkinson Series

Principal Offices of the Bank

Contemporary photographs from which the illustrations were derived.

Head Office, Edinburgh

The Commercial Bank of Scotland Limited

Glasgow: Gordon Street

London: Lombard Street

The Second Bradbury Wilkinson Series

The Second Issue

With only one printing for each denomination of the first issue completed, it was decided to modify the design and to change the basic colour of the notes to a dark shade of blue. The modification consisted of additional lithographic overlays, an oval framework surrounding each of the illustrations of the Glasgow and London offices, and a "network" design to cover the entire area of the front. There was no alteration to the back design apart from the colour.

The reason for the changes, which in no way can be said to enhance the appearance of the notes, is not recorded; but was almost certainly connected with attempts to provide a greater degree of security for notes of the series. It will be recalled that the first Bradbury Wilkinson series was printed in colours designed to secure a low contrast or "flat" appearance, thus rendering more difficult any attempt at forgery by photographic means. Now the first issue of the Second series had just the opposite quality, being boldly printed and in black ink. In fact it was the photographic forger's dream. It must be said however that no forgeries of either the first or second series have been reported, nor indeed are any recorded for the entire range of 20th century Commercial Bank notes. This surely underlines the high quality of engraving and printing and is a tribute to the security measures adopted in the production and handling of the notes.

The second issue had a life span of some fifteen years. Apart from changes relating to the signatures no other design modifications took place during that period but some serials were printed in red. There are however minor variations in shade, attributable no doubt to war-time difficulties in standardising the printing inks. None of the shade variations merit "variety" status. The War had another affect on the note issue, giving rise as it did to inflation. This becomes evident in the "numbers printed" columns.

The £1 note of the second issue is probably the earliest "Commercial" note with which the average collector will be familiar. It has survived in sufficient numbers to ensure reasonable availability. In top grades of condition it may prove difficult to obtain and merits the considerable premium asked by dealers over the valuation coding quoted in the following columns in which it is listed in grade F. As with

The Commercial Bank of Scotland Limited
most of the contemporary Scottish "square" notes in size A, collectors
should be willing to accept them in a "circulated" state with a view to
changing them later should something of better quality turn up. As the
number of collectors increases, the availability of the pre-1920 note
diminishes accordingly. Notes which only a few years ago were
relatively commonplace are now becoming surprisingly thin on the
ground.

Only the £1 note has so far been recorded in "Specimen" form, but it
seems probable that specimens of the other denominations were also
prepared.

One Pound. Size A. Blue with deep and light yellow overlays. Printed
signature of the Accountant. This second issue comprises no fewer
than four "sets" and these are dealt with separately in the listing.

Set 18. Printed signature of L. M. Mackay, Accountant, and hand-
signed on behalf of the Cashier. Serial letters in black.

					F
44.	44-1	2 Jan 1909	18/F	100,000	9
			18/G	100,000	9
			18/H	100,000	9
			18/I	100,000	9
		3 Jan 1910	18/J	100,000	9
			18/K	100,000	9
			18/L	100,000	9
			18M	100,000	9
		3 Jan 1911	18/N	100,000	9
			18/O	100,000	9
			18/P	100,000	9
			18/Q	100,000	9
	44-2	3 Jan 1910 SPECIMEN	–	20	Z

Set 19. As previous set but with serials in red, and printed signature of George Riddell, Cashier, from 19/L to 19/Q.

					VF
44.	44-3	2 Jan 1912	19/A	100,000	8
			19/B	100,000	8
			19/C	100,000	8
			19/D	100,000	8
		2 Jan 1913	19/E	100,000	8
			19/F	100,000	8
			19/G	100,000	8
			19/H	100,000	8
		2 Jan 1914	19/I	100,000	8
			19/J	100,000	8
			19/K	100,000	8
			19/L	100,000	8
			19/M	100,000	8
			19/N	100,000	8
			19/O	100,000	8
			19/P	100,000	8
		2 Jan 1915	19/Q	100,000	8

Set 20. As previous set but with serials in black. Printed signatures of L. M. Mackay, Accountant, and George Riddell, Cashier.

					VF
44.	44-4	2 Jan 1915	20/A	100,000	7
			20/B	100,000	7
			20/C	100,000	7
			20/D	100,000	7
			20/E	100,000	7
			20/F	100,000	7
			20/G	100,000	7
		3 Jan 1916	20/H	100,000	7
			20/I	100,000	7
			20/J	100,000	7
			20/K	100,000	7
			20/L	100,000	7
			20/M	100,000	7
			20/N	100,000	7
		2 Jan 1917	20/O	100,000	7
			20/P	100,000	7
			20/Q	100,000	7

Set 21. As previous set. Serial 21/A is in red but the remaining serials are in black. The printed signature of the Cashier is changed to that of H. M. Roberts during serial 21/D dated 2 January 1920.

Post-war inflationary effects are evident in the increased number of notes printed for each serial.

					VF
44.	44-5	2 Jan 1918	21/A in red	500,000	6
			21/B in black	377,500	6
		2 Jan 1919	21/C	367,000	6
		2 Jan 1920	21/D	515,000	6
			21/E	500,000	6
		3 Jan 1921	21/F	500,000	6
		3 Jan 1922	21/G	500,000	6
		2 Jan 1923	21/H	500,000	6
		2 Jan 1923	21/I	500,000	6

Five Pounds. Set 13. Size W. Hand-signed on behalf of the Accountant and the Manager. From serial 13/C dated 2 January 1913 the signature of L. M. Mackay, Accountant, is in printed form.

					F
45.	45-1	2 Jan 1909	13/A	10,000	9
		3 Jan 1910	13/A	16,000	9
			13/B	6,000	9
		3 Jan 1911	13/B	14,000	9
		2 Jan 1912	13/B	10,000	9
		2 Jan 1913	13/B	10,000	9
			13/C	10,000	9
		2 Jan 1914	13/C	10,000	9
		2 Jan 1915	13/C	5,000	9
		3 Jan 1916	13/C	10,000	9
			13/D	40,000	9
		2 Jan 1917	13/E	11,200	9
		2 Jan 1918	13/E	40,000	8
		2 Jan 1918	13/F	20,600	8
		2 Jan 1919	13/G	20,000	8
			13/H	41,200	8
		2 Jan 1920	13/I	40,000	8
			13/J	50,000	8
		3 Jan 1921	13/K	40,000	8
			13/L	20,000	8
		2 Jan 1923	13/L	20,000	8
			13/M	40,000	8

The Commercial Bank of Scotland Limited
Twenty Pounds. Set 11. Size W. Hand-signed by the Accountant and on behalf of the Manager. Between 1914 and 1917 the signature of L. M. Mackay appears in printed form.

					F
46.	46-1	3 Jan 1910	11/A	3,000	10
		3 Jan 1911	11/A	3,000	10
		2 Jan 1913	11/A	5,000	10
		2 Jan 1914	11/A	2,000	10
		3 Jan 1916	11/A	4,000	10
		2 Jan 1917	11/A	5,000	10
		2 Jan 1918	11/A	5,000	10
		2 Jan 1919	11/A	5,000	10
		2 Jan 1920	11/A	5,000	10
		2 Jan 1923	11/B	5,374	10

One Hundred Pounds. Set 10. Size W. Hand-signed by the Accountant and on behalf of the Manager. Between 1914 and 1918 the signature of L. M. Mackay, Accountant, appears in printed form.

					F
47.	47-1	2 Jan 1908	10/A	1,000	12
		2 Jan 1909	10/A	600	12
		3 Jan 1910	10/A	600	12
		2 Jan 1913	10/A	1,000	12
		2 Jan 1914	10/A	400	12
		2 Jan 1918	10/A	1,000	11
		2 Jan 1919	10/A	1,000	11
		2 Jan 1920	10/A	1,000	11
		2 Jan 1923	10/A	1,089	11

36a-2
(p. 44)

36a-2R
(p. 44)

37-2
(p. 46)

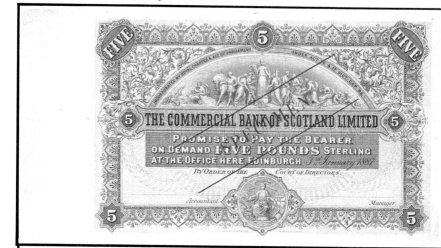

37-2R
(p. 46)

38-2
(p. 47)

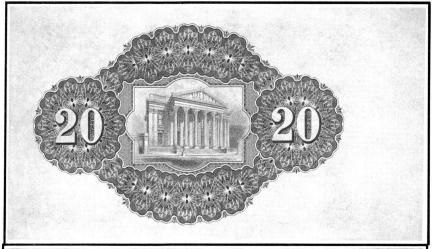

38-2R
(p. 47)

39-2
(p. 47)

39-2R
(p. 47)

40-2
(p. 49)

40-2R
(p. 49)

41-2
(p. 49)

41-2R
(p. 49)

42-2
(p. 49)

43-2
(p. 49)

44-2
(p. 53)

45-1
(p. 55)

46-1
(p. 56)

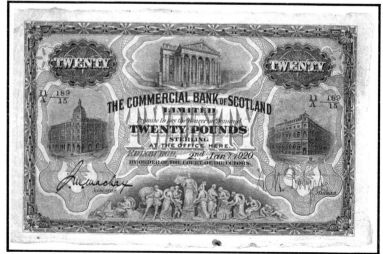

47-1
(p. 56)

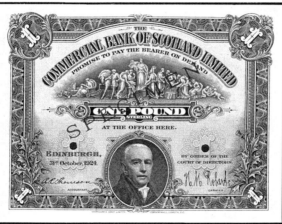

48-2
(p. 67)

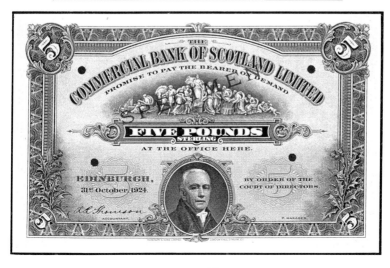

49a-2
(p. 67)

49b-1
(p. 68)

50-3
(p. 70)

51-4
(p. 71)

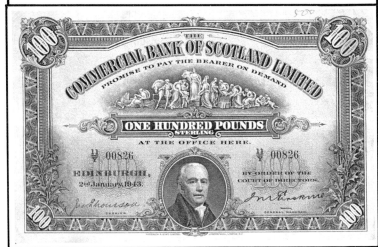

The Pitcairn Series

In 1924 new designs were prepared by Waterlow and Sons Ltd. These feature the portrait of John Pitcairn of Pitcairns, the first Chairman of the Bank, adapted from the Raeburn painting now in the Royal Scottish Academy. Known in consequence as the "Pitcairn" issue, all denominations have the same basic design, generally regarded as being one of the finest of the entire Scottish series. Apart from a reduction in size of the One Pound note in 1927 (Size B), the Pitcairn notes continued in issue until 1947, with the customary variations in signatures and serial numbers. The back design has a fine engraving of the Head Office surrounded by complex white line engraving. The basic plate is printed in dark blue for all the denominations, with a shaded yellow and red overlay on the face.

A feature of the issue is the reversed alphabetical order in which the serial letters appear, commencing at Z, although the more normal practice of commencing with the letter A was restored in the One Pound note in the reduced Size B.

Specimen Notes were prepared for each denomination. These have "Specimen" overprinted diagonally in red and are additionally punch-holed. All are dated 31st October, 1924, and have printed signatures where applicable. They are un-numbered. All values have positional code letters in the bottom left-hand corner. (See explanation under General Introduction) and are printed on un-watermarked paper.

The Raeburn painting of John Pitcairn of Pitcairns and its adoption by Waterlow and Sons Ltd. for use on the note plates.

One Pound. Set 22. Size A. Printed signatures of R. R. Thomson, Accountant, and H. M. Roberts, Cashier.

					VF
48.	48-1	31 Oct 1924	22/Z 22/Y	500,000 each	6
		31 Oct 1925	22/X	500,000	6
		1 Nov 1926	22/W	500,000	6
	48-2	31 Oct 1924 SPECIMEN		25	Z

Specimen Notes

"Waterlow" notes, including those of this bank and of other banks here and overseas are found marked "Specimen − of no value" or in similar terms with and without the Waterlow name. These are not Specimen Notes in the strict definition of the term. They were produced by the Company as examples of their work, probably for promotional purposes and were not commissioned by the banks concerned. As such they are **not** listed here, reference to Specimen Notes being restricted to those specifically ordered for that purpose by the banks and which officially form part of a particular issue. Usually these promotional notes appear in colour combinations which differ from those of the issued notes and have been described as "colour trials" in dealers' lists. This is an incorrect description.

Promotional notes of this kind are nevertheless of interest, but collectors should be aware of their proper status.

Five Pounds. Set 14. Size W. Printed signature of R. R. Thomson, Accountant and hand-signed on behalf of the Manager.

					VF
49a	49a-1	31 Oct 1924	14/Z	100,000	8
			14/Y	100,000	8
			14/X	20,000	8
		1 Nov 1926	14/X	40,000	8
			14/W	40,000	8
	49a-2	31 Oct 1924 SPECIMEN		20	Z

Alexander Robb
General Manager 1912-1932

Roydon Ritchie Thomson
Accountant 1923-1928
Cashier 1928-1940

As previous but with printed signatures of R. R. Thompson, now Cashier, and Alexander Robb, General Manager.

					VF
49b	49b-1	1 Dec 1928	14/W	40,000	8
			14/V	30,000	8
			14/U	30,000	8
		2 Dec 1929	14/T	40,000	8
		1 Aug 1931	14/S	40,000	7
			14/R	59,900	7

Similar, but with printed signatures of R. R. Thomson, Cashier, and Sir John M. Erskine, General Manager. (Sir John Erskine later became Lord Erskine of Rerrick, Governor of Northern Ireland).

					VF
49b	49b-2	30 Apr 1934	14/R	20,000	6
			14/Q	40,000	6
			14/P	20,000	6
		6 Aug 1935	14/P	20,000	6
			14/O	40,000	6
			14/N	40,000	6

James Thomson
Cashier 1940-1956

Sir John Maxwell Erskine
General Manager 1932-1953

Similar, but with printed signatures of James Thomson, Cashier, and Sir John M. Erskine, General Manager.

					GVF
49b	49b-3	20 Nov 1937	14/M	40,000	5
			14/L	40,000	5
			14/K	20,000	5
		3 Aug 1940	14/K	20,000	4
			14/J	40,000	4
			14/I	40,000	4
		3 Jun 1941	14/H	40,000	4
			14/G	40,000	4
			14/F	20,000	4
		3 Mar 1942	14/F	20,000	4
			14/E	40,000	4
			14/D	40,000	4
			14/C	40,000	4
			14/B	40,000	4
			14/A	20,000	4
		5 Jan 1943	14/A	20,000	4

Set 15. Signatures as previous.

					GVF
49b	49b-4	5 Jan 1943	15/Z	40,000	4
			15/Y	40,000	4
			15/X	40,000	4
			15/W	40,000	4
			15/V	40,000	4
			15/U	40,000	4
			15/T	40,000	4
			15/S	40,000	4
			15/R	20,000	4
		1 Dec 1944	15/R	20,000	4
			15/Q	40,000	4
			15/P	40,000	4
			15/O	40,000	4
			15/N	40,000	4
			15/M	20,000	4

Twenty Pounds. Set 12. Size W. Printed signature of R. R. Thomson, Accountant, and hand-signed on behalf of the Manager.

					F
50.	50-1	31 Oct 1924	12/Z	5,000	7
		1 May 1925	12/Z	5,000	7
	50-2	31 Oct 1924		20	Z
		SPECIMEN			

As before, but with printed signatures of R. R. Thomson, Cashier, and Alexander Robb, General Manager.

					F
50	50-3	1 May 1928	12/Z	5,000	7
		1 Dec 1928	12/Y	5,000	7
		1 Aug 1931	12/Y	4,000	7
			12/X	6,000	7

As before, but with printed signatures of R. R. Thomson, Cashier, and Sir John M. Erskine, General Manager.

					VF
50	50-4	31 July 1935	12/X	6,000	7
			12/W	4,000	7
		25 Oct 1937	12/W	8,000	7
			12/V	2,000	7

The Commercial Bank of Scotland Limited
Similar, but with printed signatures of James Thomson, Cashier, and Sir John M. Erskine, General Manager.

					VF
50	50-5	2 Aug 1940	12/V	10,000	6
		2 June 1941	12/U	5,000	6
		2 Mar 1942	12/U	2,000	6
			12/T	3,000	6
		4 Jan 1943	12/T	5,000	6
			12/S	11,000	6
			12/R	12,000	6
			12/Q	2,000	6

One Hundred Pounds. Set 11. Size W. Printed signature of R. R. Thomson, Accountant, and hand-signed on behalf of the Manager.

					F
51	51-1	31 Oct 1924	11/Z	1,000	11
		1 Dec 1928	11/Z	2,000	11
	51-2	31 Oct 1924 SPECIMEN		20	Z
		1 Dec 1928 SPECIMEN		20	Z

As above, but printed signatures of R. R. Thomson, Cashier, and Alexander Robb, General Manager.

					F
51	51-3	30 Sep 1937	11/Z	1,000	11

Similar, but printed signatures of James Thomson, Cashier, and Sir John M. Erskine, General Manager.

					GF
51	51-4	1 Aug 1940	11/Z	1,000	10
		2 Jan 1943	11/Z	2,000	10
			11/Y	2,000	10

ONE POUND: Size B: Sets 23, 24 and 25

The One Pound note was issued in 1927 in reduced format conforming to that of the then current £ 1 Treasury note. The Pitcairn design remained unaltered except where minor modification was necessary to accommodate the reduction in size. Having a life of twenty years and embracing three "sets" there are several variations in signature and serials which make this note an interesting one for collectors.

The new note was printed in sheets of 16 on unwatermarked paper and with positional code letters at bottom left corner. Specimen notes were prepared, dated 1st December, 1927 and overprinted in red. In addition there are two punch holes.

Set 23: Serial 23A

Serial letter in Gothic type. Printed signatures of R. R. Thomson, Accountant, and H. M. Roberts, Cashier.

					VF
52a.	52a-1	1 Dec 1927	?3A	1,000,000	4
	52a-2	1 Dec 1927 SPECIMEN		20	Z

Peter Irving
Chief Accountant 1928-1946

Set 23: Serials 23B and 23C

Serial letters in Gothic capitals. Printed signature of Peter Irving, Accountant, and R. R. Thomson, Cashier.

						VF
52a	52a-3	1 Jun 1928	23B		1,000,000	3
		1 Dec 1928	23B	23C	1,000,000 each serial letter	3

Set 23: Serials 23D to 23Z

Serial letters in Roman capitals. Printed signatures of Peter Irving, Accountant, and R. R. Thomson, Cashier.

						GVF
52b	52b-1	2 Dec 1929	23D		1,000,000	3
		1 Jun 1931	23E		1,000,000	2
		31 May 1932	23F 23H	23G 23I	250,000 each serial	2
		31 Jul 1933	23J	23K	250,000 each serial	2
		31 Mar 1934	23L 23N	23M 23O	250,000 each serial	2
		8 Apr 1935	23P 23R	23Q 23S	250,000 each serial	2
		12 Feb 1936	23T 23V	23U 23W	250,000 each serial	2
		30 Nov 1936	23X 23Z	23Y	250,000 each serial	2

Set 24: Serials A/24 to P/24

Printed signatures of Peter Irving, Accountant, and R. R. Thomson, Cashier.

					GVF
52c	52c-1	2 Set 1937	A/24 B/24 C/24 D/24	250,000 each serial	2
		22 June 1938	E/24 F/24 G/24 H/24 I/24 J/24 K/24 L/24	250,000 each serial	2

	4 May 1939	M/24 N/24 O/24 P/24	250,000 each serial	2

Set 24: Serials Q/24 to Z/24
Set 25: Serials A/25

Printed signatures of Peter Irving, Chief Accountant, and James Thomson, Cashier.

					GVF
52c	52c-2	6 Aug 1940	Q/24 R/24 S/24 T/24 U/24 V/24 W/24 X/24	250,000 each serial	2
		4 Jun 1941	Y/24 Z/24	250,000 each serial	2
	52c-3	4 Jun 1941	A/25	250,000	2

Set 25: Serials 25B to 25N

Number followed by triangle in solid colour. Printed signatures of Peter Irving, Chief Accountant, and James Thomson, Cashier.

					GVF
52d	52d-1	4 Jun 1941	25B 25C 25D 25E 25F	250,000 each serial	2
		6 Jan 1943	25G 25H 25I 25J	250,000 each serial	2
		2 Dec 1944	25K 25L 25M 25N	250,000 each serial	2

Serial Letters — Sets 23, 24 and 25

As the Pitcairn B-size note embraced three sets, an effort was made to distinguish each set. Set 23 had the set number preceding the serial letter in the orthodox manner, e.g. 23A. The first three letters, A, B and C were in Gothic capitals and the remainder in Roman capitals. In Set 24 the set number is placed below the serial letter and this practice is continued for the first letter of Set 25 — A/25. The procedure was then changed for the remaining serials of Set 25 reverting to that used in Set 23, but in order to distinguish it from the earlier set a triangle in solid colour was added at the end of the number. These variations provide one of the fascinating features of this particular note.

The Commercial Bank of Scotland Limited
The "Cockburn" Series

A new series of notes from plates engraved by Bradbury Wilkinson and Co. Ltd., replaced the Pitcairn series in 1947. The designs provided a break from tradition, being "modern" in concept and colour. The One and Five pound notes were in bright purple with a multi-colour facing, and the two top values were in basic colours of blue and green respectively. The choice of differing colour schemes for the higher denominations was a logical one, and it is strange that the system had not been introduced at an earlier stage. Many a Scottish banker, perhaps now happily in retirement, will recall a traumatic experience with large denominational notes of similar colour and appearance, when as a teller and at the end of a busy day, he nursed a cash "difference" occasioned as a result of wrong visual identification of such a note during a split second mental lapse. Not until the 1970s however were colour schemes standardised by all the issuing banks, by which time of course the Commercial Bank had passed into history.

The designs, by Stephen Gooden, C.B.E., R.A., who was also responsible for that of the George Medal and the "Britannia Head" Five Pound note of the Bank of England, have as the main feature a portrait of Lord Cockburn. A cameo head emblematic of Scotia is supported by figures representing Agriculture and Commerce, this head being repeated in the watermark. The back design of the "large" notes, which now appear in the reduced format of Size X, provides a further innovation. Hitherto figures on Scottish note designs were either of a classical or allegorical nature, but now they appear "live" in an engraving illustrating the Head Office and George Street as they were when the Bank first took up residence there in the 1840s.

This was the last series to be issued by the Commercial Bank, and apart from a change in the basic colour of the One Pound note in 1954 and a new signature on all denominations in the same year, it continued without other modification until 1959 when the Bank joined with the National Bank in the formation of the National Commercial Bank of Scotland Limited.

HOW
Our Bank Notes are Made

Today the Commercial Bank of Scotland has more notes in circulation than any other non-State Bank in the world.

Issued in denominations of £1, £5, £20 and £100, they are at all times popular with the public and nearly £12,000,000 of our notes are circulating in Scotland.

The notes were designed by Mr. Stephen Gooden, C.B.E., R.A., in conjunction with Messrs Bradbury, Wilkinson and Company Limited, by whom they were engraved, and printed on paper specially made by Messrs Portals Limited.

The finely engraved portrait of Lord Cockburn, the first Governor of the Bank, adds dignity to the designs and special notice should be taken of the handsome watermark which appears on all values. In these days of modern printing methods these two features, together with the artistic colour work, offer the greatest safeguard against reproduction.

To give strength and durability to the paper for our notes, only the best materials are used. The distinctive watermark is effected by the pulp and water passing over a cylindrical mould, the water passing through the wire gauze, leaving the pulp adhering to the mould and eventually being passed through blankets in the form which is known as waterleaf. Drying and sizing operations follow.

The combination of fine engraving and the beautiful colours obtained by printing from steel plates is a pleasure to the artistic eye and a classic example of the engraver's art.

Strict control of all materials and paper used during the course of manufacture is essential. Every detail must be perfect, from the original design to the finished notes.

(Acknowledgements to "The Griffin" staff magazine of The Commercial Bank of Scotland Limited, April 1949).

One Pound. Set 26. Size B. Purple with multicolour facing. Printed signature of Sir John M. Erskine, General Manager. Printed in sheets of 15 impressions.

							EF	
53	53-1	2 Jan 1947	26A	26B		1,000,000	2	
			26C	26D		each		
			26E	26F		serial		
			26G					
		3 Jan 1949	26G	26H		1,000,000	2	
			26I	26J		each		
						serial		
		3 Jan 1950	26K	26L	26M	1,000,000	2	
						each		
						serial		
		3 Jan 1951	26M	26N	26O	1,000,000	2	
						each		
						serial		
		3 Jan 1952	26P	26Q	26R	1,000,000	2	
						each		
						serial		
		2 Jan 1953	26R	26S		1,000,000	2	
			26T	26U		each		
						serial		
			26V			100,000	3	
	53-2	3 Jan 1951	No Printed			25	Z	
		SPECIMEN	signature					
			000000 26N					

Ian Wilson Macdonald
General Manager 1953-1959

Set 27. Size B. Blue with multicolour facing. Printed signature of Ian W. Macdonald, General Manager.

							EF
54	54-1	2 Jan 1954	27A 27C	27B 27D		900,000 each serial	1
		3 Jan 1955	27D 27F	27E 27G		900,000 each serial	1
		3 Jan 1956	27G 27I	27H 27J		900,000 each serial	1
		2 Jan 1957	27K 27M	27L 27N		900,000 each serial	1
		2 Jan 1958	27N	27O	27P	900,000 each serial	1
			27Q			600,000	1
		1 Jul 1958	27Q			300,000	2
			27R			730,000	2
	54-2	2 Jan 1954 SPECIMEN	000000 27A			25	Z

Five Pounds. Set 16. Size X. Purple with multicolour facing. Printed signature of Sir John M. Erskine, General Manager. Printed in sheets of 8.

					EF
55	55-1	2 Jan 1947	16A	100,000	3
			16B	80,000	3
			16C	100,000	3
			16D	120,000	3
		3 Jan 1949	16E	100,000	3
			16F	100,000	3
			16G	80,000	3
			16H	80,000	3
			16I	80,000	3
			16J	40,000	3
		3 Jan 1951	16K	80,000	3
			16L	80,000	3
			16M	80,000	3
			16N	80,000	3

The Commercial Bank of Scotland Limited

		3 Jan 1952	16O	80,000	3
			16P	80,000	3
			16Q	80,000	3
			16R	80,000	3
			16S	80,000	3
			16T	80,000	3
		2 Jan 1953	16U	80,000	3
			16V	80,000	3
			16W	80,000	3
			16X	80,000	3
			16Y	80,000	3
			16Z	80,000	3
	55-2	3 Jan 1951 SPECIMEN	16N 000000	25	Z

Set 17. Similar. Printed signature of Ian W. Macdonald, General Manager.

					EF
55	55-3	2 Jan 1954	17A	80,000	3
			17B	80,000	3
			17C	80,000	3
			17D	80,000	3
			17E	80,000	3
			17F	80,000	3
		3 Jan 1955	17G	80,000	3
			17H	80,000	3
			17I	80,000	3
			17J	80,000	3
			17K	80,000	3
			17L	80,000	3
		3 Jan 1956	17M	80,000	3
			17N	80,000	3
			17O	80,000	3
			17P	80,000	3
			17Q	80,000	3
			17R	40,000	3
		2 Jan 1957	17S	80,000	3
			17T	80,000	3
			17U	80,000	3
			17V	80,000	3
			17W	80,000	3
			17X	80,000	3
			17Y	80,000	3
			17Z	80,000	3
	55-4	3 Jan 1955 SPECIMEN	17G 000000	25	Z

Set 18. Similar.

						EF
55	55-5	2 Jan 1958	18A		80,000	3
			18B		80,000	3
			18C		80,000	3
			18D		80,000	3
			18E		80,000	3
			18F		80,000	3

Twenty Pounds. Set 13. Size X. Blue with multicolour facing. Printed signature of Sir John M. Erskine, General Manager.

						EF
56	56-1	2 Jan 1947	13A		12,000	5
			13B		12,000	5
			13C		12,000	5
			13D		6,000	5
			13E		2,000	5
		3 Jan 1950	13E		10,000	5
			13F		12,000	5
		3 Jan 1951	13G		3,000	5
		3 Jan 1952	13G		10,000	5
			13H		12,000	5
			13I		3,000	5
		2 Jan 1953	13I		10,000	5
			13J		12,000	5
			13K		3,000	5
	56-2	2 Jan 1947 SPECIMEN	13A 000000		25	Z
		3 Jan 1951 SPECIMEN	13G 000000		25	Z

Similar, but with printed signature of Ian W. Macdonald, General Manager.

						EF
56	56-3	2 Jan 1954	13K		6,000	5
			13L		9,000	5
		3 Jan 1956	13L			5
			13M		15,000	5
			13N		10,000	5
		2 Jan 1958	13N		5,000	5
			13O		10,000	5
			13P		10,000	5
	56-4	3 Jan 1956 SPECIMEN	13L 000000		25	Z

The Commercial Bank of Scotland Limited
One Hundred Pounds. Set 12. Size X. Green with multicolour facing.
Printed signature of Sir John M. Erskine, General Manager.

					GVF
57	57-1	2 Jan 1947	12A	1,000	10
		3 Jan 1951	12A	3,000	9
		2 Jan 1953	12B	3,000	9
	57-2	2 Jan 1947 SPECIMEN	12A 0000	25	Z
		3 Jan 1951 SPECIMEN	12A 0000	025	Z

THE NATIONAL
BANK OF SCOTLAND LIMITED
1825–1959

The National Bank of Scotland Limited,
42 St. Andrew Square, Edinburgh.

The National Bank purchased Dumbreck's Hotel at No. 39 St. Andrew Square and commenced business on 30th October, 1825. In 1835 the adjoining property at No. 42 was purchased and this served as the Head Office until 1936. After a spell in temporary premises to enable a larger office to be constructed, the doors of 42 St. Andrew Square opened again for business in June 1942. The Architects of this commodious building, which has continued as a Head Office notwithstanding two mergers, were Arthur Davis RA and Lester Grahame-Thomson, RSA FRIBA.

THE NATIONAL BANK OF SCOTLAND LIMITED

Founded in 1825, it had by the end of the 19th century developed a branch system extending throughout Scotland and was the first of the Scottish banks to open in London. Its progress during the first half of the present century was uneventful until in 1918 its share capital was acquired by Lloyds Bank Limited. Although it maintained a close relationship with the English bank it operated quite independently until 1959 when it joined with The Commercial Bank of Scotland Limited in forming National Commercial Bank of Scotland Limited. The Head Office in St. Andrew Square, Edinburgh is now the administrative headquarters of The Royal Bank of Scotland plc. The colourful note issue with its numerous design and signature variations has proved a popular field for collectors.

The note issue*

The striking — and somewhat flamboyant — series first introduced in 1893 continued into the present century until 1908 when minor modifications were made to the design. The Marquess of Lothian whose portrait was the dominant feature of the notes was no longer Governor, and the caption beneath the portrait was amended to show the dates during which he had held office and now occupies two lines of print. The Manager was re-designated General Manager and this change is reflected in the signature details. Otherwise the designs remain unchanged and apart from signature variations continued in issue until 1934 when the Royal Arms were replaced by those of the Bank. The One Pound note however was completely re-designed in 1927 appearing in reduced size (Size B).

The National Bank of Scotland Limited

Technical Details: Designed, printed, and engraved by Waterlow and Sons Ltd., on unwatermarked paper. Four denominations: One Pound (Size A) and Five Pounds (Size W) in blue with yellow and red overlay, Twenty and One Hundred Pounds (Size W) in similar shades but with a bright pink overlay.

Specimen Notes. Dated and undated specimen notes were produced for all denominations.

R.W.P.

The highly complex design of this series — particularly the high values — has long been a favourite with collectors, and it may be of interest to identify the various vignettes which comprise it.

*The Royal Arms of Scotland
later to be replaced by those
of the Bank.*

The National Bank of Scotland Limited

*Edinburgh Castle
as seen from the Mound.*

*Shipping on the River Clyde,
Glasgow*

*The Palace of Holyrood House,
Edinburgh.*

*View of Edinburgh from Carleton Hill
(back design)*

The National Bank of Scotland Limited
The notes are printed in blue from the engraved plate and have a yellow and red lithographic overlay in the form of a sunburst in the £ 1 note, and a discreet floral design in the higher denominations. The £ 20 and £ 100 notes have an additional overlay in pink.

One Pound note of the first type (caption under portrait in one line). Two proxy signatures, one printed Thomas Shaw p. Manager and one in manuscript p. Accountant. Engraved by Waterlow and Sons Ltd., London.

				GF
20	20-1	2 Jan 1893	A	10
		1 Jan 1898		10
		1 Jan 1903	D	9
		2 Jan 1905	D	9
	20-2	1 Jan 1898		Z
		SPECIMEN		
		(in red)		

Five Pound note of the first type, 21. Two proxy signatures, both in manuscript, p. Accountant and p. Manager. Specimens undated and punched, and printed "SPECIMEN" in red. First issued 2 Jan 1893.

Twenty pound note of the first type, 22, with pink overlay. Signatures and specimens as for the five pound note.

Hundred pound note of the first type, 23, with pink overlay. Two manuscript signatures of the Manager and the Accountant. Specimens as for the five pound note.

One Pound
One Pound note of the second type (caption under portrait in two
lines). Printed signature of W. Samuel on behalf of the General
Manager and signed on behalf of the Accountant. Small modifications
made to the plates.

				GF
24	24-1	15 May 1908	F	9
		11 Nov 1910	F	8
				VF
		15 May 1911	F	7
		11 Nov 1911	G	7
		15 May 1912	G	7
		11 Nov 1912	G	7
		15 May 1913	G	7
		11 Nov 1913	G	7
		15 May 1914	G	7
		1 Aug 1914	H	7
		15 May 1915	H	7
		1 Oct 1915	H	7
		11 Nov 1915	H,J	7
		15 May 1916	J	7
		11 Nov 1916	J	7
		15 May 1917	J, K	7
		12 Nov 1917	K	7
		15 May 1918	K	7
		11 Nov 1918		7
		15 May 1919	L	7

Printed signatures W. Samuel p. General Manager and A.
McKissock, Accountant (The 11 Nov 1919 issue reads p. Accountant).

				VF
24	24-3	11 Nov 1919	L	7
		24 May 1920	L	7
		8 Jul 1920		7
		11 Nov 1920		7
		11 Nov 1921		7
		11 Nov 1922	M	7
		15 May 1923	M	7
		15 May 1924	N	7
	24-4	11 Nov 1919		Z
		SPECIMEN		

Printed signatures of William Lethbridge, Cashier, and Andrew McKissock, Accountant.

				VF
28	28-1	15 May 1925	N	6
		2 Jan 1926	N, O	6
		1 Jul 1926	O	6

W. Samuel
General Manager

Andrew McKissock
Accountant

Five Pounds

Five Pound note of the second type (Caption under portrait in two lines). Hand-signed on behalf of the General Manager and the Accountant. Imprint Waterlow and Sons Limited, London, England.

				F
25	25-1	15 May 1909	A	8
		11 Nov 1913	A	8
		1 Aug 1914	A	8
		15 May 1916	A	8
		15 May 1917	A	8
		12 Nov 1917	A	8

52a-2
(p. 72)

52a-2R
(p. 72)

52a-3
(p. 73)

53-1
(p. 77)

53-1R
(p. 77)
also

54-1R
(p. 78)
but in blue colour

54-1
(p. 78)

55-1
(p. 78/79)

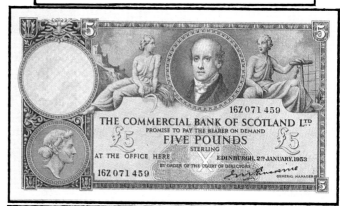

56-1
(p. 80)

56-1R
(p. 80)

57-1
(p. 81)

The National Bank of Scotland Limited

20-1
(p. 86)

20-1R
(p. 86)

21-2
(p. 86)

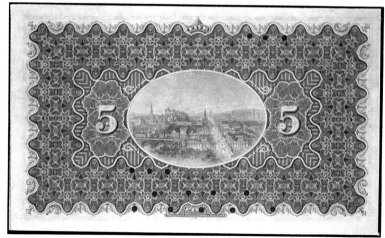

21-2R
(p. 86)

also

29-1R
(p. 97)

22-2
(p. 86)

23-2
(p. 86)

24-1
(p. 87)

29-1
(p. 97)

26a-1
(p. 97)

32-3
(p. 99)

32-3R
(p. 99)

33-1
(p. 100)

36-4
(p. 106)

37-2
(p. 107)

39-2
(p. 109)

39-2R
(p. 109)

The National Bank of Scotland Limited

Printed signature of W. Samuel of behalf of the General Manager and hand-signed on behalf of the Accountant.

				GF
25	25-3	11 Nov 1919	A	8
		8 July 1920	A	8
	25-4	11 Nov 1919		Z
		SPECIMEN		

Printed signature of William Lethbridge, Cashier, and hand-signed on behalf of the Accountant.

				GF
29	29-1	1 Jul 1927	A	8
		2 Jul 1928	A	8
		11 Nov 1930	A	7

Printed signature of George Drever, Cashier, and hand-signed on behalf of the Accountant.

				VF
29	29-2	11 Nov 1932	A	7

Twenty Pounds

Hand-signed on behalf of the General Manager and of the Accountant. Bright pink overlay.

				F
26a	26a-1	1 Aug 1914	A	10

Printed signature of Wm. Lethbridge, Cashier, and hand-signed on behalf of the Accountant.

				GF
30	30-1	1 Mar 1928	A	10
		2 Jan 1930	A	10

Printed signature of George Drever, Cashier, and hand-signed on behalf of the Accountant.

				VF
30	30-2	11 Nov 1932	A	9

One Hundred Pounds

Hand-signed on behalf of the General Manager and of the Accountant. Bright pink overlay.

				VF
27	27-1	16 May 1935	A	10

Printed signature of Wm. Lethbridge, Cashier, and hand-signed on behalf of the Accountant.

31	31-1

The One Pound Note — Size B

In conformity with the decision of the Scottish banks to reduce the size of the One Pound note to that corresponding to the then current Treasury Note, a new "National" note appeared in 1927 in colours which were a complete departure from tradition. The basic plate was printed in black, but the addition of yellow, orange, and red overlays — the latter in the form of a sunburst — conveys an overall brown effect. Indeed brown was the shade selected for printing the back design. The new design reflects something of the character of its predecessor, retaining the Royal Arms as a central feature, flanked now by vignettes of Glasgow Cathedral (left) and the Palace of Holyroodhouse (right). The notes were designed, engraved and printed as before by Waterlow and Sons Ltd. The back design retains as the central motif a view of Edinburgh from Calton Hill similar to that featured in the previous £1 note, but the surrounding white-line framework has been completely re-designed. Micro code letters indicative of Waterlow notes are included.

Notes of this basic design remained in issue until the merger with The Commercial Bank of Scotland in 1959 — a period of 32 years. There were however several modifications and signature variations, during the lengthy period of issue and these have made the series a popular and challenging one for collectors. Minor colour variations occasioned by changes in the shades of the overlay tones occur over the years but these are not of sufficient importance to warrant according them "variety" status.

Generally the later printings have brighter and more contrasting overlay shades and the red tones predominate.

The National Bank of Scotland Limited

In 1934 the Royal Arms were replaced by those of the Bank and during the currency of the series we have a change in the printing process and three different printers' imprints.

Technical Details: Designed engraved and printed by Waterlow and Sons Ltd., and later printed by W. and A. K. Johnston Ltd., subsequently W. and A. K. Johnston and G. W. Bacon Ltd. Printed signature of the Cashier and later the General Manager. Positional code letters on the Waterlow printings.

Specimen Notes: These varied in form with different printings.

Glasgow Cathedral　　　　　*Palace of Holyroodhouse*

One Pound

Waterlow

Printed signature of William Lethbridge, Cashier.

					GVF
32	32-1	2 Nov 1927	A/A	1,000,000	3
		2 Jul 1928	A/B	1,000,000	3
		1 Nov 1929	A/C	1,000,000	3

Printed signature of George Drever, Cashier.

					GVF
32	32-3	2 Feb 1931	A/D	1,000,000	4

Joint print figure for Waterlow & Johnston printings.

The Johnston Printings

In 1931 it was decided to have the One Pound note printed locally in Edinburgh. There were obviously sound administrative advantages to be derived from this but at that time none of the Edinburgh printing establishments was equipped to print large quantities of notes by the line engraved process hitherto in use. W. and A. K. Johnston Ltd., were however in a position to print by means of a deep-offset litho process which was considered a suitable alternative and so the printing of the One Pound note passed to them. The other values were left in Waterlow's hands. The new printing, which is identical in design, is distinguishable by its "flatter" appearance and the absence of finer detail in the white-line work due entirely to the different process. The notes now bear the imprint of W. and A. K. Johnston and do not have the positional code letters present in the Waterlow printings.

In 1953 W. and A. K. Johnston Ltd. merged with another firm of Edinburgh printers to form a new company "W. and A. K. Johnston and G. W. Bacon Ltd.". and from then the imprint appears in that form.

W. and A. K. Johnston Ltd.
Printed signature of George Drever, Cashier.

					GVF
33	33-1	2 Feb 1931	A/D	1,000,000 Joint print figure for Waterlow & Johnston printings.	4
		11 Nov 1932	A/E	1,000,000	3
		11 Nov 1933	A/F	1,000,000	3

Third Type: The Royal Arms replaced by those of the Bank.

In common with the notes of the Bank of Scotland and The British Linen Bank, the Royal Arms of Scotland were replaced in 1934 by new Arms specially prepared for the Bank. The Royal Arms had been a feature of the notes for well over a century and had been included by virtue of the Royal Charter granted to the Bank. It is strange that no exception had been taken until then by successive Lords Lyon, but the Lord Lyon King of Arms reigns supreme in matters of heraldry in Scotland and his edicts are obeyed without question. As was the case

The National Bank of Scotland Limited

with The British Linen Bank the simple expedient of replacing the Royal Arms with those of the Bank leaving the design of the note otherwise unchanged solved the problem. It is doubtful if the general public even noticed the alteration but the directors were now absolved from the dire consequences under the old Scottish Law of their action in aiding the unauthorised display of the Royal Arms of Scotland.

The modification was applied to all denominations of the current series. Otherwise the technical details remain unaltered.

Speciment Notes: A small number (of each denomination) of the issued notes was set aside, overprinted, and utilised as "Specimens". Punch holes were applied to the spaces containing the numbers.

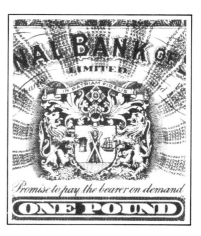

Royal Arms of Scotland   *The Bank's Arms*

The many signature variations of the Five Pound Note are a feature of this Issue.

One Pound

Bank Arms: W. and A. K. Johnston Ltd. Printed signature of George Drever, Cashier.

					GVF
34	34-1	12 Nov 1934	A/G	1,000,000	3
		1 Aug 1935	A/H		3
		15 Apr 1936	A/I		3
		2 Jan 1937	A/J		3
		3 Aug 1937	A/K		3
		3 May 1938	A/L		3
		7 Nov 1938	A/M		3
		1 Jun 1939	A/N		3
		20 Nov 1939	A/O		3
		31 Jul 1940	A/P		2
		1 May 1941	A/Q		2
		23 Oct 1941	A/R		2
		1 May 1942	A/S		2

Printed signature of John T. Leggat, General Manager W. and A. K. Johnston Ltd.

				GVF
38a	38a-1	15 Mar 1943	A/T	2
		1 Nov 1944	A/U	2
		15 Jun 1946	A/V	2

Printed signature of J. A. Brown, General Manager W. and A. K. Johnston Ltd.

				GVF
38a	38a-2	1 Mar 1947	A/W	2
		1 Nov 1947	A/X	2
		31 Jul 1948	A/Y	2
		30 Apr 1949	A/Z	2
		1 Dec 1949	B/A	2
		1 Jun 1950	B/B	2
		4 Jan 1951	B/C	2
		5 Jul 1951	B/D	2
		24 Jan 1952	B/E	2
		1 Jul 1952	B/F	2
		2 Jan 1953	B/G	2
	38a-3	4 Jan 1951 SPECIMEN Number cut out. Two punch holes.	B/C	Z

Printed signature of J. A. Brown, General Manager. W. and A. K. Johnston and G. W. Bacon Ltd.

				GVF
38b	38b-1	1 Jun 1953	B/H	2
		11 Nov 1953	B/I	2
		1 Jun 1954	B/J	2
		1 Oct 1954	B/K	2

Printed signature of David Alexander, General Manager. Designation in Roman capitals.

				EF
38b	38b-2	1 Mar 1955	B/L	2
		16 Jul 1955	B/M	2
		3 Jan 1956	B/N	3

Designation "General Manager" in italics.

				EF
38b	38b-3	3 Jan 1956	B/N	3
		10 May 1956	B/O	2
		1 Oct 1956	B/P	2
		15 Jan 1957	B/Q	2
		28 Mar 1957	B/R	2
		1 Jun 1957	B/S	2
		1 Aug 1957	B/T	2
		30 Nov 1957	B/U	2
		1 Mar 1958	B/V	2
		1 May 1958	B/W	2
		1 Jul 1958	B/X	2
		1 Oct 1958	B/Y	2
		2 Feb 1959	B/Z	2
		1 May 1959	C/A	3

Five Pounds

a) Vertical Setting of Signatures

Printed signature of George Drever, Cashier, and hand-signed on behalf of the Accountant.

				GVF
35	35-1	1 Jul 1936	A B	3

Printed signatures of A. A. Bremner, Accountant, and George Drever, Cashier.

				GVF
35	35-2	1 Aug 1939	B	3
		1 Jul 1940	B	3
		1 Mar 1941	B	3

Printed signatures of A. A. Bremner, Chief Accountant (in larger style), and George Drever, Cashier.

				GVF
35	35-3	6 Jul 1942	B	3

b) Horizontal Setting of Signatures
Printed signatures of John T. Leggat, General Manager, and George Drever, Cashier.

				GVF
35	35-4	11 Jan 1943	B	3

Printed signatures of John T. Leggat, General Manager, and A.S.O. Dandie, Cashier.

				GVF
35	35-5	3 Jan 1944	B	3
		1 Jun 1944	B	3
		2 Jan 1945	B	3
		2 Jan 1945	C	3

The National Bank of Scotland Limited

Printed signatures of J. A. Brown, General Manager, and A.S.O. Dandie, Cashier.

				GVF
35	35-6	3 Jun 1947	C	3
		1 Sep 1948	C	3
		1 Nov 1949	C	3
		1 Feb 1951	C	3
		1 Mar 1952	C	3
		3 Jan 1953	C	3
		3 Jan 1953	D	3
		1 Oct 1953	D	3
		1 May 1954	D	3
	35-7	1 Nov 1949 SPECIMEN numbers cut out and punch holes.	C	Z

In the last two printings, the brown overlay is more pronounced.

Printed signatures of David Alexander, General Manager, and A.S.O. Dandie, Cashier.

				EF
35	35-8	1 Jul 1955	D	3
		1 Dec 1955	D E	3
		31 Dec 1956	E	3

John T. Leggat
General Manager

Twenty Pounds

a) Vertical Setting of Signatures
Printed signature of George Drever, Cashier, and hand-signed on behalf of the Accountant.

				VF
36	36-1	16 May 1935	A	5
		1 Jul 1936	A	5
		1 Aug 1939	A	5
		1 Apr 1941	A	5

Printed signature of A. A. Bremner, Chief Accountant, and hand-signed on behalf of the Cashier.

				VF
36	36-2	8 Dec 1941	A	5
		6 Jul 1942	A	5

b) Horizontal Setting of Signatures
Printed signatures of John T. Leggat, General Manager, and A.S.O. Dandie, Cashier.

				VF
36	36-3	1 Jun 1944	A	5
		2 Jan 1945	A	5

Printed signatures of J. A. Brown, General Manager, and A.S.O. Dandie, Cashier.

				GVF
36	36-4	2 Jun 1947	A	5
		1 Nov 1949	A	5
		1 Feb 1951	A	5
		1 Mar 1952	A	5
		1 May 1954	A	5
	36-5	2 Jun 1947 SPECIMEN numbers cut out and punch holes.	A	Z

The National Bank of Scotland Limited

Printed signatures of David Alexander, General Manager, and A.S.O. Dandie, Cashier.

				GVF
36	36-6	31 Dec 1956	A	5

One Hundred Pounds

a) Vertical Setting of Signatures

Printed signatures of George Drever, Cashier, and John T. Leggat, General Manager.

		VF
37	37-1	10

b) Horizontal Setting of Signatures

Printed signatures of John T. Leggat, General Manager, and George Drever, Cashier.

				VF
37	37-2	11 Jan 1943	A	10

Printed signatures of J. A. Brown, General Manager, and A.S.O. Dandie, Cashier.

				GVF
37	37-3	2 Jun 1947	A	10
		1 Nov 1949	A	10
		1 Mar 1952	A	10
	37-4	1 Nov 1949	A	Z
		SPECIMEN numbers cut out and punch holes.		

Printed signatures of David Alexander, General Manager, and A.S.O. Dandie, Cashier.

		GVF
37	37-5	9

THE NATIONAL
BANK OF SCOTLAND LIMITED
NEW NOTES

The National Bank of Scotland Limited intimate that their Notes of the £5, £20 and £100 denominations have been re-designed to conform to modern practice in regard to size. The new Notes, which will be issued as from 20th January, 1958, have been designed and printed by Messrs Waterlow and Sons Limited, London, who have made use of a special paper prepared by Messrs Portals Limited, incorporating a watermark in the form of a portrait of the first Chairman of the Bank, Sir Alexander Henderson of Press, a former Lord Provost of Edinburgh and Master of the Merchant Company, who played a prominent part in the development of the City in the early years of the Nineteenth Century.

The face of the Notes bears a reproduction of the Bank's Coat of Arms and incorporates the Scottish thistle and a variety of other designs, while on the back there is an impression of the forth bridge, the selection of which has no particular significance beyond providing an immediately recognisable Scottish scene and at the same time a clear layout, which would present difficulties to any would-be forger.

As regards tinting, all three denominations have a lithographic "rainbow" background with dates, signatures, and serial numbers in black letter-press, while the main printing is by the Intaglio process, the £5 Notes being in green, the £20 Notes in red, and the £100 Notes in blue.

It is not intended meantime to change the design of the Bank's £1 Notes which are printed in Edinburgh by Messrs W. and A. K. Johnston and G. W. Bacon Limited.

January 1958

The Press Notice reproduced above, provides details of the new "large" notes introduced in 1958. The back design of the Forth Railway Bridge is the forerunner of the long series of "Bridge" motifs which continued through the National Commercial Bank issues to the first notes of The Royal Bank of Scotland. The three denominations are in Size X.

Specimen Notes. Overprinted "Specimen" and with two small punch holes. Each value numbered A 000-000.

Printed signatures of David Alexander, General Manager and A.S.O. Dandie, Cashier.

Five Pounds

				EF
39	39-1	1 Nov 1957	A B	3
	39-2	1 Nov 1957 SPECIMEN A 000-000	A	Z

Twenty Pounds

				EF
40	40-1	1 Nov 1957	A	5
	40-2	1 Nov 1957 SPECIMEN A 000-000	A	Z

One Hundred Pounds

				GVF
41	41-1	1 Nov 1957	A	8
	41-2	1 Nov 1957 SPECIMEN A 000-000	A	Z

In 1959 The National Bank of Scotland Limited merged with The Commercial Bank of Scotland Limited to form The National Commercial Bank of Scotland Limited.

THE NATIONAL COMMERCIAL
BANK OF SCOTLAND LIMITED
1959 — 1969

Head Office of the National Commercial Bank of Scotland Limited
42 St. Andrew Square, Edinburgh

NATIONAL COMMERCIAL BANK OF SCOTLAND LIMITED

When in 1950 The Clydesdale Bank joined with the Aberdeen-based North of Scotland, the arrangement seemed logical geographically and the merger had little effect on Scottish banking as a whole. Five years later when the Bank of Scotland acquired the Union Bank this was a different matter. Each had country-wide branch systems so geography has little to do with this merger. It was prompted by a desire to rationalise administration and resources by creating a larger bank. On the horizon lay the prospects of electronic accounting with consequent large capital outlays and further mergers were inevitable. In 1959 The Commercial Bank of Scotland Limited, which had the largest branch system and the largest note circulation in the country joined with The National Bank of Scotland Limited to form National Commercial Bank of Scotland Limited, in its lifetime Scotland's largest bank. Its existence however was a relatively short one of ten years duration as in 1970 the new bank linked with the old The Royal Bank of Scotland in an even greater merger, forming The Royal Bank of Scotland Limited.

The Note Issue

To a collector desiring to "complete" the issues of one of the Scottish banks, National Commercial afford a unique opportunity. Having during its short reign the largest note circulation in the country, the notes are still readily available and, apart from "Specimen" notes, there are no rarities. There are but eleven face and signature different notes with a total face value of £ 154, but this small collection can be considerably expanded by the inclusion of date and serial variations. Having stated that there are no rarities it must be admitted that one or two of the notes are becoming increasingly difficult to find.

The First Issue

The first notes attempt to preserve the traditions of both constituent banks. The One Pound note is in the style and colour of the last Commercial Bank note of that denomination. It was also designed, engraved and printed by Bradbury Wilkinson and Co. Limited. It makes one concession to the former National Bank by incorporating as its motif an illustration of the Forth Railway Bridge which was featured in the last issue of that bank. This bridge appears in all but two of the National Commercial designs and its inclusion has no greater significance other than the provision of a suitable Scottish landmark of the correct proportions for the oblong format of the notes. There is one interesting "error" in the illustration of the Bridge. The shipping channel lies between the second and third arches whereas the ship on the engraving is shown negotiating the tricky waters between the first and second. The error was rectified on the redesigned One Pound note of 1968. The three higher denominations have many of the characteristics of the previous National Bank "large" notes — including the large illustration of the Forth Bridge on the back design — and their production was entrusted to the same engravers, Waterlow and Sons Ltd.

Technical Details: One Pound: blue with multicolour facing: Size B. Designed, engraved and printed by Bradbury Wilkinson and Co. Ltd. The watermark consists of the head of Caledonia. Printed signature of the General Manager.

Five Pounds: Green and multicolour, Twenty Pounds: Red and multicolour.

One Hundred Pounds: Purple and multicolour — all Size X — designed, engraved and printed by Waterlow and Sons Limited. Printed signature of the General Manager.

Specimen Notes:

All Denomination: Overprinted "Specimen" in red, back and front, and perforated "Specimen".

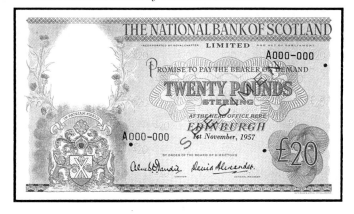

40-2
(p. 109)

41-2
(p. 109)

National Commercial Bank of Scotland Limited

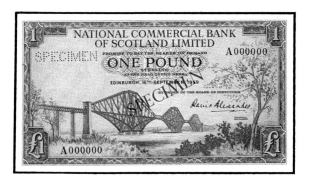

1-2
(p. 121)

1-2R
(p. 121)

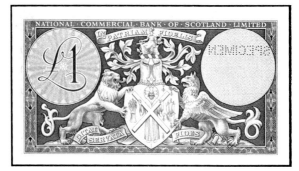

2-2
(p. 122)

2-2R
(p. 122)

3a-2
(p. 122)

3a-2R
(p. 122)

4a-2
(p. 123)

4a-2R
(p. 123)

5-2
(p. 123)

5-2R
(p. 123)

6a-2
(p. 125)

6a-2R
(p. 125)

7a-2
(p. 125)

7a-2R
(p. 125)

8-2
(p. 126)

8-2R
(p. 126)

6b-2R
(p. 127)

7b-2R
(p. 127)

National Commercial Bank of Scotland Limited

9-2
(p. 128)

9-2R
(p. 128)

The Royal Bank of Scotland

46c-1
uniface
(p. 130)

46d-1
uniface
(p. 131)

47-1
(p. 132)

47-2
(p. 133)

David Alexander
General Manager
(1959-1968)

Also General Manager, National Bank
1956-1959.

1959

One Pound. Blue with multicolour facing. Designed, engraved and printed by Bradbury Wilkinson and Co. Ltd. Printed signature of David Alexander, General Manager. Size B.

					EF
1	1-1	16 Sep 1959	A B C D E F G H I J K L M N P Q R S T U V W X Y Z 1A 1B 1C 1D 1E 1F	1,000,000 each serial	2
	1-2	16 Sep 1959 SPECIMEN A 000000	A	50	Z

Five Pounds. On the face at the bottom of the note towards the right appears the Coat of Arms of the Bank. Through an oval window towards the left appears a watermark based on a portrait of the Right Honourable Alexander Henderson of Press, at one time Lord Provost of the City of Edinburgh and first Chairman of the Board of Directors of the National Bank of Scotland Limited. Green with multicolour facing. Designed, engraved and printed by Waterlow and Sons Ltd. Printed signature of David Alexander, General Manager. Size X.

					EF
2	2-1	16 Sep 1959	A B C D E F	1,000,000 each serial	3
			G	550,000	4
	2-2	16 Sep 1959 SPECIMEN A 000000	A	50	Z

Twenty Pounds. Red with multicolour facing. Designed, engraved and printed by Waterlow and Sons Ltd., for the 1959 issue. The 1967 issue was printed by Thomas de la Rue, who had taken over from Bradbury Wilkinson. Printed signature of David Alexander, General Manager. Size X.

					EF
3	3a-1	16 Sep 1959	A	350,000	5
	3b-1	1 June 1967	A	100,000	X
	3a-2	16 Sep 1959 SPECIMEN A 000000	A	50	Z
	3b-2	1 June 1967 SPECIMEN A 000000	A	50	Z

Although the records show that 3b-1 was printed and issued in the number shown, no dealer or collector has seen it. Perhaps the notes were recalled and destroyed when the Bank became the Royal Bank Limited within a short time of the printing. Specimen 3b-2 does exist.

One Hundred Pounds. Purple with multicolour facing. Designed, engraved and printed by Waterlow and Sons Ltd., for the 1959 issue. The 1967 issue was printed by Thomas de al Rue, who had taken over from Bradbury Wilkinson. Printed signature of David Alexander, General Manager. Size X.

					GVF
4	4a-1	16 Sep 1959	A	25,000	9
	4b-1	1 June 1967	A	15,000	X
	4a-2	16 Sep 1959 SPECIMEN A 000000	A	50	Z
	4b-2	1 June 1967 SPECIMEN A 000000	A	50	Z

Comment on 4b-1 is as for 3b-1. No dealer or collector has seen it. Specimen 4b-2 does exist.

The watermark on the One Pound note is the cameo head of Scotia featured in the Commercial Bank notes while that on the higher denominations is the portrait of Alexander Henderson from the final "large" notes of the National Bank. We can assume therefore that the new bank made good use of the quantity of banknote paper which must have been on hand at the time of the merger.

Reduction in size of the Five Pound note

In January 1961 the Five Pound note was issued in reduced size (Size Y). In basic design and colour it is similar to the earlier note but with some minor modifications, particularly to the frame lines. Designed engraved and printed by Waterlow and Sons Limited. This was a short-lived issue, being replaced in 1963 by an entirely new design.

Five Pounds. Green with multicolour facing. Printed by Waterlow and Sons Ltd. Size Y.

					EF
5	5-1	3 Jan 1961	G	450,000	4
			H	1,000,000	3
			J	350,000	4
	5-2	3 Jan 1961 SPECIMEN G 000000	G	200	Z

It is interesting that the above serial letter G is shared with G of the 2-1 series of 16 September, 1959 i.e. in notes of different sizes (X and Y) and dates.

National Commercial Bank of Scotland Limited
New designs in Standardised Colours

November 1961 saw the introduction of a new One Pound note in Size C and in the standardised green colour agreed by all banks. The main features of the earlier design were retained. This was followed in January 1963 by a Five Pound note of entirely new design, Size Z, and in the standard shade of blue. No change took place in the Twenty and One Hundred Pound notes which continued in their original design and colours until the Merger in 1969. The Five Pound note in the new design was engraved and printed by Bradbury Wilkinson and Co. Ltd.

Shown below is the official Press Notice covering the issue of the two new notes.

As from 24th January, 1963, a new £5 note is being brought into circulation by the National Commercial Bank. The dimensions of the note will be the same as the Bank of England £5 one, to be introduced shortly, and it is intended that all Scottish notes of this denomination will eventually conform to this standard size. The design of the new note, which is predominantly blue in colour, differs from the existing issues in many respects, but particularly noticeable is the substitution on the reverse side of a view of Edinburgh Castle and the Art Galleries for that of the Forth Railway Bridge. These notes will circulate along with the existing £5 notes meantime but the Bank state that they intend to effect withdrawal of the former issues later in the year.

Last year National Commercial Bank introduced a new green £1 note which at present circulates side by side with an earlier larger blue note of the same value. The latter was gradually being withdrawn but it has now become possible for the process to be speeded up.

National Commercial Bank of Scotland Limited

One Pound. Green with multicolour facing. Designed, engraved and printed by Bradbury Wilkinson and Co. Ltd. Printed signature of David Alexander, General Manager. Size C.

					EF
6a	6a-1	1 Nov 1961	A B C D E F G H	1,000,000 each serial	1
		1 Nov 1962	J K L M N P Q R S T	1,000,000 each serial	1
		1 Aug 1963	U V W X Y Z 1A 1B 1C 1D 1E 1F	1,000,000 each serial	1
		1 Oct 1964	1G 1H 1J 1K 1L 1M 1N 1P 1Q 1R 1S 1T	1,000,000 each serial	1
		4 Jan 1966	1U 1V 1W 1X 1Y 1Z 2A 2B 2C 2D 2E 2F	1,000,000 each serial	1
	6a-2	1 Nov 1961 SPECIMEN A 000000	A	50	Z

Five Pounds. Blue and multicolour. Printed by Bradbury Wilkinson and Co. Ltd. Printed signature of David Alexander, General Manager. Size Z.

					EF
7a	7a-1	2 Jan 1963	A B C	1,000,000 each	2
		1 Aug 1963	D E F	1,000,000 each	2
		1 Oct 1964	G H	1,000,000 each	2
		4 Jan 1966	J K	1,000,000 each	2
			L	400,000	2
		1 Aug 1966	L	600,000	2
			M	1,000,000	2
			N	800,000	3
	7a-2	2 Jan 1963 SPECIMEN A 000000	A	50	Z
		1 Oct 1964 SPECIMEN G 000000	G	5	Z

National Commercial Bank of Scotland Limited

Ten Pounds. During the 20th century there was little demand in Scotland for a note of this denomination. Neither the Commercial nor the National Banks had included it in any of their note issues for almost a hundred years. Banks which did found little public support for the Ten Pound note. However, in the 1960s the increasing incidence of inflation coupled with the introduction of the Bank of England note of this denomination influenced the Scottish banks to add it to their current series. It was by no means an instant success, and the numbers circulating fell far short of those of the Twenty Pound note at the outset.

The design on the front of the National Commercial note is similar to that of the Five Pound note of 1963 but the new standard shade of brown was utilised in the printing. The outstanding feature of the note however is in the back design which keeps alive the "bridges" tradition by illustrating the newly-opened Tay Road Bridge with a panorama of Dundee in the background. A nice little gesture is the dating of the note — 18th August 1966 — the date of the official opening of the Bridge.

					GVF
8	8-1	18 Aug 1966	A	500,000	4
	8-2	18 Aug 1966 SPECIMEN A 000000	A	5	Z

In 1967 both values were encoded as explained in the following Press Notice. This entailed minor modifications to the back designs in order to accommodate the symbols.

ENCODED BANK NOTES

National Commercial Bank is now issuing £1 notes with special markings in the form of seven small horizontal bars approximately 3mm by 0.1mm, printed on the back of the notes in each of two "windows" or small areas of paper 7mm by 9mm which are clear of the printing used in the general design of the note. £5 notes similarly encoded will be introduced at an early date. In neither case will there be any other change in the design of the notes.

These code bars will be used to sort notes by machines under development for the Scottish Banks, which they expect will be introduced about the end of next year. In pioneering this development, the aim of the Banks is to increase their efficiency by doing away with the need to sort and count their notes by hand. These machines will operate at a speed of 600 notes per minute.

21st October, 1967.

One Pound. Similar to previous issue but back modified to accommodate the encoding symbols. Printed signature of David Alexander, General Manager.

					EF
6b	6b-1	4 Jan 1967	2G 2H 2J 2K 2L 2M 2N 2P 2Q 2R 2S 2T	1,000,000 each serial	1
	6b-2	4 Jan 1967 SPECIMEN 2G 000000	2G	50	Z

John B. Burke
General Manager
(1968-1969)

Also General Manager and Managing
Director, Royal Bank plc 1969-82

Five Pounds. Printed signature of John B. Burke, General Manager. Encoded for electronic sorting.

					EF
7b	7b-1	4 Jan 1968	N	200,000	3
			P Q	1,000,000	2
			R	200,000	3
	7b-2	4 Jan 1968 SPECIMEN N 000000	N	5	Z

Note the sharing of the N serial of the Burke signature with the N serial of the Alexander signature (1 August 1966).

According to the Bank and the Printers records, it was intended that these notes be dated 1 Nov. 1967. The late date change was due to the change of General Manager.

National Commercial Bank of Scotland Limited
The One Pound note in Size D

This final issue of National Commercial Bank £ 1 note appeared after the announcement of the proposed merger had been made public as explained in the following Press Notice. Since the previous One Pound note showed no trace of the Forth Road Bridge, opened in 1964, steps were taken to introduce this in the background. The ship is now navigating the proper channel The note is also reduced in size (Size D) and is encoded, but other technical details are unchanged.

NEW £1 NOTE

On Monday, 2nd December 1968, the National Commercial Bank of Scotland Limited will issue a smaller £1 note of the same colour but differing slightly in design on the front from the present one. The note is identical in size to the proposed Bank of England £1 note.

The front of the note, which is green in colour, continues to feature the Forth Railway Bridge but has been redesigned so as to bring into view in the background the Forth Road Bridge.

The reverse, which is also green in colour, shows the Bank's Coat of Arms.

The National Commercial, which will merge with The Royal Bank of Scotland next year, had this note at an advanced stage of production before the merger negotiations were concluded and it is now being put into circulation as existing supplies of the note which it supersedes have been used up.

One Pound. Size D. with printed signature of John B. Burke, General Manager. Encoded.

					EF
9	9-1	4 Jan 1968	A B C D E F G H J(?) K	1,000,000 each serial	1
	9-2	4 April 1968 SPECIMEN A 000000	A	50	Z

The Bank records show that A-R were printed, but that L-R were destroyed and never issued, as the Royal Bank Limited was being formed. However, no dealer or collector has yet recorded the J issue. Was this perhaps destroyed?

THE ROYAL BANK OF SCOTLAND
1727-1969

The Royal Bank of Scotland, 36 St. Andrew Square, Edinburgh.

Designed by Sir William Chambers of Ripon and built between 1772 and 1774 as the town house of Sir Laurence Dundas of Kerse, then M.P. for Edinburgh. This House became the principal office of the Excise for Scotland and was bought by the Royal Bank of Scotland in 1825. It continued as the Head Office of the Bank until the merger between the Royal Bank and the National Commercial Bank. The building now houses the St. Andrew Square banking office of The Royal Bank of Scotland plc.

THE ROYAL BANK OF SCOTLAND
Founded 1727
Together with the National Commercial Bank of Scotland Limited formed the Royal Bank of Scotland Limited in 1969

A brief history of the Bank is given in earlier pages; we will confine ourselves here to a discussion of the note issue.

At the turn of the century the blue and brown £1 notes of the Royal Bank in circulation were those of the series first issued in 1875. The basic design, dating back to 1832, consisted of a portrait of George I flanked by the unicorn and the lion of the Royal Arms. The seated figure of Britannia and the standing figure representing Plenty holding a cornucopia are on the left and right of the note. The uniface notes were engraved on steel by W. and A. K. Johnston Limited, and from 1887-1907 bore the printed signature of W. Templeton, Accountant, and an additional manuscript signature. The background of a light brown network over the whole area of the note is practically invisible.

One Pound. Size A. 1887-1907.

Printed signature W. Templeton, Accountant, and hand-signed on behalf of the Cashier. Blue and brown. The new serial letters starting in 1900 are in Gothic capitals.

					F
46c	46c-1	2 Feb 1888	P		11
		12 Jul 1888			11
		2 Jan 1895	U	400,000	10
			V	400,000	10
			W	400,000	10
			X	400,000	10
			Y	400,000	10
			Z	400,000	10
		1 Nov 1900	A	400,000	10
			B	400,000	10
		2 Jan 1903	C	400,000	10
			D	400,000	10
			E	400,000	10
			F	400,000	10
		?.? 1907	G	400,000	10
		3 Jan 1908	H	Joint print figure with 46d-1 'H'	10

The Royal Bank of Scotland
One Pound. Size A. 1908-1926

Printed signature of D. S. Lunan, Accountant, and hand-signed on behalf of the Cashier. Serial letters in Gothic capitals. The brown network is now either absent or almost invisible.

					F
46d	46d-1	5 May 1908	H	400,000	10
		14 Jan 1909	H		
		13 Oct 1909	I	400,000	10
					VF
		5 May 1910	K	400,000	7
		2 Nov 1910	K		
		2 May 1911	L	400,000	7
		2 Sep 1911	M	400,000	7
		1 Apr 1912	M		
		2 Jan 1913	N	400,000	7
		8 Jan 1914	O	400,000	7
		16 Jul 1914	P	400,000	7
		30 Dec 1914	Q	400,000	7
		1 Jul 1915	R	400,000	7
		24 Dec 1915	S	400,000	7
		25 Jul 1916	T	400,000	7
		10 Mar 1917	U	400,000	7
		1 Sep 1917	V	400,000	7
		2 Feb 1918	W	400,000	7
		29 Jun 1918	X	400,000	7
		20 Feb 1919	Y	400,000	7
		29 Jun 1919	Z	400,000	7
		24 Mar 1920	A (in red as below).	110,000	7

Printed signature of David Speed, Accountant, and hand-signed on behalf of the Cashier. Serial letters in red Roman capitals.

					VF
46c	46c-1	14 May 1920	A	290,000	7
					GVF
		11 Nov 1920	B	400,000	6
		24 Mar 1921	C	400,000	6
		29 Jun 1921	D	400,000	6
		20 Feb 1922	E	400,000	6
		28 Aug 1922	F	400,000	6
		24 Mar 1923	G	400,000	6
		7 Jul 1923	H	400,000	6

				GVF
20 Feb 1924	I		400,000	6
29 Oct 1924	J		400,000	6
14 May 1925	K		400,000	6
25 Nov 1925	L		400,000	6
14 May 1926	M		400,000	6

This was a remarkable series to have remained in issue for so long with only minor modifications and one which offers wonderful scope for specialisation.

An essay by W. and A. K. Johnston exists with a similar basic design but printed in multicolour with an illustration of the Bank's Head Office on the back also printed in several colours. This is dated 7 July 1913. A finely engraved essay by Bradbury Wilkinson and Co. Ltd. is dated 1914. Further essays exist dated 1921 submitted by Waterlow and Sons Ltd.

In common with other Scottish banks the £ 1 note was issued in reduced size in 1927. The basic features of the "Lizars" note were retained, but with a printed back containing illustrations of the Head Office and the principal office in Glasgow in circular panels. The note is printed by a deep-etch offset process with a lithographic overlay in reddish-brown. It has a printed signature of David Speed, the Accountant, and is additionally hand-signed on behalf of the Cashier. This is the last Scottish note to have a manuscript signature. Imprint W. and A. K. Johnston Ltd., Edinburgh.

One Pound. Size B.

Blue and red-brown with an almost invisible pale yellow underlay. Printed signature of David Speed, Accountant, and hand-signed on behalf of the Cashier. Serial letter follows the number (black). Watermark now reversed when viewed from the front, probably due to a change in paper and note making machinery.

					VF
47	47-1	2 Feb 1927	A (Suffix)	275,000	5

Note: 275,000 is the number obtained from the official Bank Records; However the actual number issued must be less than 127,000 according to evidence produced by the collectors, and the number of 47-2 prefix A notes is correspondingly higher than the figure tabled.

As previously, but serial letter precedes the number (blue).

					VF
47	47-2	2 Feb 1927	A (prefix)	724,799	4
		30 Nov 1927	B	999,500	4
		15 Oct 1928	C	999,500	4
		14 Oct 1929	D	999,500	4
		18 Oct 1930	E	999,500	4
		11 Nov 1931	F	999,500	4
		31 Oct 1932	G	999,500	4
		31 Oct 1933	H	999,500	4
		31 Oct 1934	J	999,500	4
		31 Oct 1935	K	999,500	4
		24 Dec 1936	L	31,500	5

Printed signature of David Steel, now signing as Chief Accountant. The overlay ranges from a very pale shade in the early printings to yellow. The unique 1 September 1939 issue with A suffix is of interest.

					GVF
48a	48a-1	2 Jan 1937	A/1	999,500	3
		3 Jan 1938	B/1	999,500	3
		1 Dec 1938	C/1	999,500	3
		1 Sep 1939	D/1	999,500*	3
		1 Sep 1939	D/1....A	16,000	
			Only one postively known to have survived.		
		1 Sep 1940	E/1	999,500	3
		1 Sep 1941	F/1	999,500	3
		1 Jul 1942	G/1	999,500	3

*The [D/1....A] issue of 1 September, 1939, runs from serial number D/1 847, 701 A to D/1 866, 700 A, but covers only 16,000 notes in this range. These serial numbers duplicate numbers in the normal D/1 series. It is not clear why the [D/1....A] issue exists. However, as the actual issue by the Bank was on 18 July, 1940, it seems likely that a duplication error in the printed numbers had taken place and the introduction of the A suffix on the duplicate notes was means of avoiding the wastage of 16,000 notes at a time of material shortages.

Printed signature of T. Brown, Chief Accountant.

					GVF
48b	48b-1	1 Mar 1943	H/1	999,500	2
		6 Jan 1944	J/1	999,500	2
		1 Dec 1944	K/1	999,500	2
		24 Jan 1946	L/1	999,500	2
		6 Jan 1947	M/1	999,500	2
		1 Oct 1947	N/1	999,500	2
		11 Oct 1948	O/1	999,500	2
		1 Oct 1949	P/1	999,500	2
		1 Jun 1950	R/1	999,500	2
		2 Jan 1951	S/1	999,500	2
		1 Jul 1951	T/1	265,000	2

Printed signature of J. D. C. Dick, Chief Accountant.

					EF
48c	48c-1	16 Jul 1951	U/1	999,500	2
		1 Feb 1952	V/1	999,500	2
		2 Jun 1952	W/1	999,500	2
		1 Nov 1952	X/1	999,500	2

J. D. C. Dick,
Chief Accountant
1951-54
Assistant General Manager
1954-65

Imprint changed to W. and A. K. Johnston and G. W. Bacon Ltd., Edinburgh.

					EF
48d	48d-1	1 Apr 1953	Y/1	999,500	2
		1 Aug 1953	Z/1	999,500	2

New system of serial numbers. Larger signature.

					EF
48d	48d-2	1 Dec 1953	AA	999,500	2
		1 Apr 1954	AB	999,500	2
		1 Jul 1954	AC	999,500	2
		1 Oct 1954	AD	999,500	2
		3 Jan 1955	AE	999,500	2

As previously, but deeper blue and much more pronounced yellow background. Printed signature of W. R. Ballantyne as General Manager.

					EF
49	49-1	1 Apr 1955	AF	999,500	1
		1 Aug 1955	AG	999,500	1
		1 Nov 1955	AH	999,500	1
		1 Feb 1956	AJ	999,500	1
		1 Jun 1956	AK	999,500	1
		1 Sep 1956	AL	999,500	1
		1 Dec 1956	AM	999,500	1
		1 Mar 1957	AN	999,500	1
		1 Jul 1957	AO	999,500	1
		1 Oct 1957	AP	999,500	1
		1 Feb 1958	AQ	999,500	1
		1 Apr 1958	AR	999,500	1
		1 Aug 1958	AS	999,500	1
		1 Nov 1958	AT	999,500	1
		2 Feb 1959	AU	999,500	1
		1 Apr 1959	AV	999,500	1
		1 Sep 1959	AW	999,500	1
		2 Nov 1959	AX	999,500	1
		1 Mar 1960	AY	999,500	1
		1 Jun 1960	AZ	999,500	1
		1 Sep 1960	BA	999,500	1
		1 Nov 1960	BB	999,500	1

				EF
	1 Feb 1961	BC	999,500	1
	1 Apr 1961	BD	999,500	1
	1 Jun 1961	BE	999,500	1
	2 Oct 1961	BF	999,500	1
	2 Jan 1962	BG	999,500	1
	1 Mar 1962	BH	999,500	1
	1 May 1962	BI	999,500	1
	1 Aug 1962	BJ	999,500	1
	1 Oct 1962	BK	999,500	1
	2 Jan 1963	BL	999,500	1
	2 Apr 1963	BM	999,500	1
	1 Jun 1963	BN	999,500	1
	2 Sep 1963	BO	999,500	1
	2 Dec 1963	BP	999,500	1
	2 Mar 1964	BQ	999,500	1
	1 May 1964	BR	999,500	1
	1 Jul 1964	BS	999,500	1
49-2	SPECIMEN			

W. R. Ballantyne
General Manager
1953-1965

Design as before, but size reduced to C. Printed signature of W. R. Ballantyne, General Manager.

					EF
51a	51a-1	1 Aug 1964	CA	999,500	1
		2 Nov 1964	CB	999,500	1
		1 Dec 1964	CC	999,500	1
		1 Mar 1965	CD	999,500	1
		1 Apr 1965	CE	999,500	1
		1 May 1965	CF	999,500	1
		1 Jun 1965	CG	999,500	1
	51a-2	SPECIMEN 1 Aug 1964 CA 000000	CA		Z

Printed signature of G. P. Robertson, General Manager.

					EF
51b	51b-1	2 Aug 1965	CH	999,500	1
		1 Oct 1965	CI	999,500	1
		1 Dec 1965	CJ	999,500	1
		3 Jan 1966	CK	999,500	1
		1 Feb 1966	CL	999,500	1
		1 Mar 1966	CM	999,500	1
		1 Apr 1966	CN	999,500	1
		1 Jun 1966	CO	999,500	1
		1 Jul 1966	CP	999,500	1
		1 Oct 1966	CQ	999,500	1
		3 Jan 1967	CR	999,500	1
		1 Mar 1967	CS	999,500	1
		1 May 1967	CT	999,500	1
		1 Jun 1967	CU	999,500	1
		1 Jul 1967	CV	999,500	1
		1 Sep 1967	CW	999,500	1
		1 Nov 1967	CX		1

The last two dates overlap those of the next issue.

Five Pounds. Size W.

The basic designs were prepared in 1861 and 1877 by W. and A. K. Johnston Ltd. of Edinburgh. These incorporate the Royal Arms flanked by words and figures of the value and a vertical panel at the left of the note. Very pale yellow overlay. Printing from the engraved plate is in blue, and a lithographic overlay in red is superimposed on the legend panel. The Bank's title is in Gothic letters. The number is printed. The last of the D series, $D\frac{2200}{10000}$ was issued on December 26, 1907, the total number of notes in the series being 440,000.

Series E. Hand-signed on behalf of the Accountant and Cashier. Uniface. Date inserted by hand. Imprint of W. and A. K. Johnston Ltd., Edinburgh. The issue ran from $E\frac{1}{1}$ (Dec 23, 1909) to $E\frac{5780}{6000}$ (Aug 13, 1942), the total number of E series notes being 1,156,000.

		Examples of dates inserted by hand	Examples of corresponding numbers	F
42b	42b-1	1 Aug 1914	E $\frac{313}{2554}$	6
		1 Mar 1917	E $\frac{468}{3435}$	6
		1 Aug 1918		6
		3 Jan 1922		6

Printed signature of David Speed, Accountant. Hand-signed on behalf of Cashier. Date printed.

		Examples of printed dates	Examples of corresponding numbers	GF
42b	42b-3	29 June 1923	E $\frac{1836}{7652}$	6
		2 Feb 1925	E $\frac{2110}{1893}$	6
		24 May 1926		6
		1 Dec 1926		6
		30 Nov 1927		6
		14 Oct 1929		6
		1 Jun 1931		6
		1 Dec 1936		6
		3 Jan 1938	E $\frac{4195}{8864}$	6

		GF
3 Jan 1939		6
		VF
1 Jun 1940		6
10 Jan 1942	E $\frac{5230}{5872}$	6

Series F. Signatures of Cashier and General Manager (initially William Whyte and afterwards I. M. Thomson) and Chief Accountant (initially D. Speed and later T. Brown) lithographed. The yellow overlay becomes much deeper later in the series. The series ran from F $\frac{1}{1}$ (14 Aug 1942) to $\frac{4473}{4578}$ (22 Nov 1951).

		Examples of printed dates		VF
42b	42b-5	1 Jul 1942	F $\frac{259}{1685}$	6
				EF
		1 Mar 1943	Total	4
		2 May 1944	number of	4
		1 Jul 1947	notes in the	4
		1 Mar 1949	series	4
		1 Mar 1950	894,578	4
		16 Oct 1950		4
	42b-6	SPECIMEN	F $\frac{4388}{7507}$	Z
		(in red)		
		Punch holes reading PAID 16 Oct 1950		

Series G. Size X.

The £ 5 note was reduced in size on 2 January, 1952. The design and other details are similar to the previous issue, except that in 1954 there were three signatures, two being those of the joint Cashiers and General Managers and the third of the Chief Accountant. The series extended from G $\frac{1}{1}$ to G $\frac{34887}{7400}$ (15 Sep 1964), the total number of notes issued being 6,977,400.

Printed signatures of I. M. Thomson and J. D. C. Dick.

				EF
			Examples of numbering	
50a	50a-1	2 Jan 1952		3
		1 Jul 1952		3
		1 Dec 1952		3
		1 May 1953		3
		1 Jul 1953	G $\frac{4787}{7275}$	3

				EF
50a-2	SPECIMEN 2 Jan 1952 Punch holes.		G $\frac{128}{5401}$	Z

Imprint of W. and A. K. Johnston and G. W. Bacon Ltd. Printed signatures of W. A. Watt, W. R. Ballantyne and J. D. C. Dick.

			EF	
			Examples of numbering	
50b	50b-1	1 Jul 1953	G $\frac{5222}{4227}$	3
		1 Feb 1954	G $\frac{6594}{8642}$	3

Printed signatures of W. R. Ballantyne and A. G. Campbell.

			EF	
			Examples of numbering	
50b	50b-3	1 Apr 1955	G $\frac{10158}{1444}$	3
		30 Apr 1956		3
		1 Mar 1957		3
		1 Apr 1958		3
		2 Mar 1959		3
		3 May 1960		3
		1 Apr 1961		3
		2 Jan 1962		3
		3 Jan 1963	G $\frac{32691}{8170}$	3

Series H. Size Z.

The £ 5 note was issued in size Z on 2 November 1964. The design is similar to that of the previous issue. The series runs from $H\frac{1}{1}$ to $H\frac{9600}{10000}$ corresponding to 1,920,000 notes.

Printed signatures of W. R. Ballantyne and A. G. Campbell.

			EF	
			Examples of numbering	
52a	52a-1	2 Nov 1964	H $\frac{5786}{7099}$	3
	52a-2	SPECIMEN 2 Nov 1964	H $\frac{0000}{0000}$	Z

47-2R
(p. 133)
also

48a - 1R to 49-1R
(p. 133) inclusive (p. 136)

also

51a-1R to 51b-1R
inclusive
but in reduced size
(p. 137)

48a-1
(p. 133)

51a-1
(p. 137)

42b-1
uniface
(p. 138)

42b-6
(p. 139)

50b-1
uniface
(p. 140)

43a-1
uniface
(p. 145)

44b-1
uniface
(p. 146)

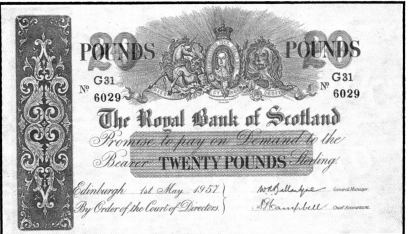

44d-3
(p. 147)

45b-1
uniface
(p. 147)

53-1
(p. 149)

53-1R
(p. 149)

54-2
(p. 149)

54-2R
(p. 149)

Printed signatures of G. P. Robertson and A. G. Campbell.

			EF	
			Examples of numbering	
52b	52b-1	2 Aug 1965	H $\frac{8097}{9268}$	3
		1 Oct 1965	H $\frac{8570}{3978}$	3

Ten Pounds. Size W.

Design details very similar to those for the £ 5 note of series E and F. Uniface.

Series C. Hand-signed and dated on behalf of the Accountant and Cashier. Blue and red. with yellow network overlay almost invisible. The series was issued in the period 1877-1917 with a total of approximately 50,000 notes. Shown are examples of the handwritten dates.

			F	
43a	43a-1	3 Mar 1914	less than	
		1 Aug 1914	2000 notes	11
		10 Apr 1917	after 1910	

Series D. Hand-signed and dated on behalf of the Accountant and Cashier. Blue and red with yellow overlay. The blue is much darker than in plate C. There were only three printings: 1916 (10,000), 1921 (10,000) and 1938 (4,000). Shown are examples of the handwritten dates. The last note in the series is numbered D $\frac{120}{4000}$

				GF
43b	43b-1	5 April 1921		8
		1 Sep 1924		8
		10 Oct 1925		8
		2 Feb 1927		8
		4 Jul 1931		8
		3 Jan 1935	24,000	8
		4 Jan 1937		8
		1 Oct 1937		8
		4 Jan 1938		8
		1 Aug 1940		8
	43b-2	1 Aug 1940 SPECIMEN numbered		Z

The Royal Bank of Scotland
Twenty Pounds. Size W.

Design details similar to those for the £ 5 and £ 10 notes. The C series (44a) existed from 1877-1912, and had a very pale overlay. The number of notes in the series was approximately 98,000. Although $C\frac{485}{6989}$ was dated 3 April, 1911, it was printed in 1905.

The **D series**, with a slightly more positive yellow overlay, ran from 1912 to 1947. The total number of notes in the series was 95,279 and the last serial number $D\frac{477}{5279}$. The date was handwritten as also were the signatures on behalf of the Accountant and Cashier. Examples of the handwritten dates are given below.

				GF
44b	44b-1	7 Jan 1931		7
		4 May 1934		7
		31 Oct 1934		7
		1 Jun 1936		7
		11 Apr 1939		7
				VF
		1 Jun 1940	95,279	6
		1 Jul 1940		6
		1 Oct 1941		6
		23 Jul 1942		6
		4 Jan 1943		6
		23 Dec 1946		6
		2 Jan 1947		6

The **E series** was similar, but the signatures of the Cashier and General Manager (I. M. Thomson) and Chief Accountant were both printed as was the date. The total number of notes in the series was 22,000 and the last serial number $E\frac{97}{9400}$

				VF
44c	44c-1	1 Jul 1947		6
		1 Oct 1949	22,000	6
		1 May 1951		5
		2 Jul 1951		5

The **F series** existed from 1 December 1952. The total number of notes issued was 20,890 and the final note was $F\frac{118}{3490}$. The Chief Accountant was J. D. C. Dick.

				VF
44d	44d-1	1 Dec 1952	20,890	5

The **G series** ran from 1 May 1957, the imprint being W. and A. K. Johnston and G. W. Bacon Ltd. The total number of notes issued was 26,800 and the final note in the series was $G\frac{134}{6800}$ The printed signatures were of W. R. Ballantyne and A. G. Campbell

				VF
44d	44d-3	1 May 1957	26,800	5

The **H series** ran from June 1966, when 10,000 notes were issued with serial numbers up to $H\frac{50}{10,000}$ until 1969.

		VF
44d	44d-5	5

One Hundred pounds. Size W.

Design details similar to those for the £ 5, £ 10 and £ 20 notes. The C series (45a) which ran from 1877 to 1912 reached a total of 30,000 notes, issued in books of 200. The notes had a very pale overlay.

The D series. Ran from 1912 to 1949. The total number of notes in this series was 8,000 and the last serial number was $D\frac{40}{8000}$ The dates were handwritten as also were the signatures on behalf of the Accountant and Cashier. Examples of handwritten dates and serial numbers are given below.

				GF
				GF
45b	45b-1	1 Sep 1937	D $\frac{31}{6186}$	10
		1 Jul 1940	D $\frac{40}{7936}$	10
		1 Aug 1940	D $\frac{39}{7704}$	10

The **E series** ran from 1949 to 1952, the total number of notes being 1073 and the last serial number $E\frac{6}{1073}$. The overlay was much more ditinctly yellow and the date and signatures of I. M. Thomson (Cashier and General Manager) and T. Brown (Chief Accountant) were printed.

					GF
45c	45c-1	1 Oct 1949	E	1073	9

In the **F series** the imprint was W. and A. K. Johnston and G. W. Bacon Ltd., and the notes had the signatures of W. R. Ballantyne (General Manager) and A. G. Campbell (Chief Accountant).

					VF
45d	45d-1	1 Oct 1960	F	500	9

In the **G series** the printed signatures were those of G. P. Robertson and A. G. Campbell.

					VF
45d	45d-2	3 Feb 1966	G	500	9

In the whole period 1912-1969 a total of 10,073 notes of the £ 100 denomination were issued, only 2,073 of these being in the twenty years from 1949-1969.

THE ONE POUND NOTE IN SIZE D

THE FIVE POUND NOTE IN SIZE Z

In 1966 the first change in basic design for over 130 years took place, the opportunity being taken to incorporate the best elements of security printing. The new notes were designed and engraved by Bradbury Wilkinson and Co. Limited and are very attractive indeed, the £ 5 note being considered by some to be the finest of modern Scottish issues. This note features a large portrait of David Dale, the Bank's first agent in Glasgow, with the Bank Arms in five colours in a panel at the right. The basic colour is blue but there is a multicolour background. The back has a large illustration of the Head Office. The £ 1 note, issued in the following year, is of the same general design but in green and multicolour. The back illustrates the Head Office and the chief office in Glasgow. It also incorporates magnetic sorting marks. The portrait of David Dale is repeated in the watermark. Both notes have steel strips.

The Royal Bank of Scotland
One Pound. Size D.
Printed signature of G. P. Robertson, General Manager. First issued 11 March 1968.

					EF
53	53-1	1 Sep 1967	A/1 to A/24	1,000,000 each number	1
	53-2	1 Sep 1967 SPECIMEN A/1 000000	A		Z

Five Pounds. Size Z
Printed signatures of G. P. Robertson, General Manager, and A. G. Campbell, Chief Accountant.

					EF
54	54-1	1 Nov 1966 1 Mar 1967	J/1 and J/2 J/3, J/4 J/5	1,000,000 each number	3
	54-2	1 Nov 1966 SPECIMEN J/1 000000	J/1		Z

The Royal Bank of Scotland merged with the National Commercial Bank of Scotland Limited in 1969 to form the Royal Bank of Scotland Limited, the notes of which must be distinguished from the foregoing issues.

NUMBER OF NOTES OUTSTANDING

The number of notes still outstanding in any particular issue is always of great interest to collectors. Unfortunately the great increase in the note circulation over the past few decades has made it impossible for the banks to segregate the various issues in arriving at a figure for outstanding notes and they now record only the over-all total.

The Royal Bank did maintain records relative to individual issues until 1966 and those for unstamped notes are listed below. Readers will appreciate that the figures given are those of notes outstanding in 1966. A large proportion of these will have been withdrawn in the normal way over the following three years and after the merger with the National Commercial Bank any further notes presented would be retained for destruction. The figures quoted are of value as an indication of the proportion of outstanding notes relative to the various issues and serials. Obviously those issued during the years immediately prior to 1966 are represented by large numbers.

Royal Bank notes in hand or in circulation
at 31st December, 1966

UNSTAMPED NOTES			FIRST STRUCK	LAST STRUCK	NUMBER
£ 100	Plate	1 or A	1854	1861	2
		2 or B	1861	1876	1
		3 or C	1876	1912	10
		4 or D	1912	1940	792
		5 or E	1949	1960	761
		6 or F	1960	1966	494
		7 or G	1966		500
£ 20		1 or A	1854	1861	12
		2 or B	1861	1875	29
		3 or C	1875	1913	122
		4 or D	1914	1947	8,893
		5 or E	1947	1952	9,999
		6 or F	1952	1957	15,587
		7 or G	1957	1966	24,199
		8 or H	1966		10,000
£ 10		1 or A	1854	1861	25
		2 or B	1862	1877	17
		3 or C	1877	1917	79
		4 or D	1917		3,247
£ 5	Plates	1 to 6	1854	1951	25,686
	Plate	7 or G	1952	1964	484,196
		8 or H	1964	1966	1,322,400
£ 1		W. Turnbull	1875	1878	7,084
		F. A. Mackay	1878	1887	8,660
		W. Templeton	1887	1908	19,318
		D. S. Lunan	1908	1920	10,188
		D. Speed	1920	1927	7,377
		A − Z/1	1927	1953	453,820
		AA onwards	1953	1964	1,069,997
		CA onwards	1964		13,060,000